DENNY AND DUNIPACE
ROLL OF HONOUR

TO
THE MEN OF
DENNY
AND
DUNIPACE
WHO FELL
IN THE GREAT WAR
1914–1918.

Denny and Dunipace Roll of Honour

The Great War
1914-1918

INTRODUCTION

CENTURY after century this Britain of ours,

> Heated hot with burning fears,
> And bathed in baths of hissing tears,
> And battered with the strokes of doom
> To shape and use,

has risen with indomitable spirit, facing every wind, ready to fight to the death any one who interfered with her in her determination to see for herself and act for herself.

This "Roll of Honour" is offered as a tribute to the men of Denny and Dunipace who, through the dark years which followed August 1914, went out, inspired by the spirit of their race, to guard the paths of the sea, to die in the trenches of France and Flanders, in Egypt, in Mesopotamia, on the barren rocks of Gallipoli, and elsewhere on the far-flung battle front. They stood the storm and the strife, and to-day our land is free of the menace of foreign domination.

The individuals may be forgotten in the years to come, but what these men did shall live for evermore. They did not leave their country to founder, and rot, and fall to pieces —as so many said she was doing. They believed that their land was worth fighting for—that it was a good land. That it may be a land worth living in should be the earnest desire and constant endeavour of all.

Every care has been taken to make the "Roll" complete. It has been found difficult to trace, and to secure particulars

5

regarding, all the men who during the years of war left the district to serve in the various branches of the Navy, the Army and the Air Forces. Young unmarried men in lodgings left none to retain a record of their going. The families of others removed from the town, and in a year or two were practically forgotten. It is thus inevitable that men whose names ought to be on the Roll are not there, but to these unknown and unrecorded heroes, as well as to those whose names it contains, the Roll is offered in tribute.

This Roll of Honour contains the names of 902 men who at time of enlistment had their homes in Denny or Dunipace.

Of these 154 were killed in action or died on Service.

Decorations were earned by 31 men.

The War Widows in the district number 39, and the War Orphans 88.

Sixteen men of the district passed lengthened periods in the hands of the enemy as Prisoners of War.

Their name liveth for evermore.

KIPLING.

List of the Fallen

whose names appear on the War Memorial.

Argyll and Sutherland Highlanders.

BAIRD, Sergt. JONATHAN
BAIRD, L/Corporal WILLIAM J.
BENNIE, Signaller CHARLES
BLACKIE, Private JAMES
BROCK, Private GEORGE FLEMING
CLEMENT, Private JAMES
CLEMENT, Private PETER
CRAWFORD, Private DAVID
CUNNINGHAM, L/Corporal JOHN
DAWSON, Private JOHN
DRYSDALE, Private JAMES
DUNNIGAN, Private JAMES
DURHAM, Private WILLIAM
GILLESPIE, Private WILLIAM HENDERSON
HEENAN, Private LAWRENCE
KEDDIE, Private WILLIAM
KERR, Sergt. ANDREW A.
KERR, Private GEORGE
KERR, Private THOMAS HILL
LORIMER, Private ALEXANDER
McARTHUR, Private JAMES
McEWAN, Signaller ALEXANDER
McGEACHIE, Private JOHN

McGLADE, Sergt.-Major JOHN
McKENZIE, Private HENRY T.
McNEIL, Private JOSEPH
NEILSON, Private ALEXANDER
NEILSON, Private JOHN MacLAREN
NEISH, Lieut. ALEXANDER MILLAR, M.C.
PARK, L/Corporal JOHN
PLANNER, Piper LEONARD
RAE, Sergt. JAMES
ROBERTSON, L/Corporal JOHN
SCOTT, Private ALBERT
SHARP, Private JAMES
SMITH, Private DANIEL
STEWART, Private ALEXANDER
THOMSON, Private JAMES
THOMSON, Corporal JOHN
TUNSTALL, Sergt. JOHN, M.M.
TURNBULL, Private HENRY
WRIGHT, L/Corporal JAMES
WRIGHT, Private JOHN

Cameron Highlanders.

DEWAR, Private WILLIAM
FORFAR, Private JAMES
HIGGINS, Private JOHN
STEWART, Private ALEXANDER
STEWART, Private JOHN ROUGH
THURSBY, Private ROBERT
WALKER, Private HENRY

Coldstream Guards.

HALKETT, Private DAVID

Dorset Regiment.

SMITH, Private ALEXANDER
TENNANT, Private DANIEL

East Lancashire Regiment.

SCOTT, Private JAMES H.

Gordon Highlanders.

BEDFORD, Private THOMAS F.
BRODIE, Private JAMES
BROWN, Corporal ABRAHAM
COYLE, L/Corporal JOHN
CUNNINGHAM, L/Corporal JAMES
DONALDSON, Private DAVID
DONALDSON, Private JAMES
FORBES, L/Corporal ALEXANDER CLARK
GILLESPIE, Private WILLIAM
LOCKHART, Private JOHN W.
MACKIE, Private ROBERT C.
McKENZIE, Private ARCHIBALD WHITE
McNEIL, Private PATRICK
MILLAR, Private JAMES
PATERSON, L/Corporal DAVID DOUGLAS
WHYTE, L/Corporal ROBERT

Grenadier Guards.

ANDERSON, Private DAVID

Highland Light Infantry.

BLACK, Private ALEXANDER B.
BLAIR, Private JAMES
HARRIS, Private HARRY
SINCLAIR, Private EDWARD
WEIR, Private WILLIAM
WILSON, Private ALEXANDER
WRIGHT, Private WILLIAM

Irish Guards.

McGRORTY, Private PATRICK

King's Own Scottish Borderers.

MITCHELL, Private JOHN
MITCHELL, Sergt. SAMUEL
MITCHELL, Private WILLIAM McNAIR

Leinster Regiment.

CONROY, Private THOMAS

Lovat Scouts.

MARSHALL, Private WILLIAM

Machine Gun Corps.

COYLE, Private JOSEPH
EASTON, Private JAMES McC.
GRANT, Private ARTHUR
HILLHOUSE, Sergt. ROBERT
MITCHELL, Gunner JAMES H.

Northumberland Fusiliers.

BUSBY, L/Corporal DUNCAN M'N.
COMRIE, Private JAMES
DUNION, L/Corporal JAMES
MURRAY, Private MICHAEL

North Lancashires.

LAWRENCE, Lieut. JAMES

R. A. S. C.

BROPHY, Driver WILLIAM

Royal Dublin Fusiliers.

COYLE, Private JAMES
CURRAN, Private DENNIS
McCULLOCH, Private JOHN
SWEENEY, Private PATRICK

Royal Engineers.

GILLESPIE, Sapper ROBERT
STEWART, Sapper GEORGE
THOMSON, Sapper JAMES

Royal Field Artillery.

KAY, Driver JOHN F.
LAMBERT, Gunner CHARLES GRAHAM, M.M.
LOCHHEAD, Fitter Staff-Sergt. ROBERT ALLAN

Royal Flying Corps.

WHYTE, Lieut. ERNEST

Royal Garrison Artillery.

ASHWOOD, Bombardier WILLIAM

Royal Highlanders.

ALLAN, Signaller L/Corporal THOMAS R.
CUMMING, Corporal GEORGE
FERGUS, Private JAMES
GRAY, Private WILLIAM A.
HANNAY, Private PETER
LORIMER, Private ALFRED
SCOBIE, Private JOHN McD.

Royal Irish Rifles.

McATEER, Private PATRICK
MULLAN, Rifleman JOHN

Royal Munster Fusiliers.

MURPHY, L/Corporal PATRICK
NEILSON, L/Corporal JAMES
O'HANLON, Private EDWARD

Royal Scots.

ANDERSON, Private GEORGE
FRASER, Private JAMES
HERMISTON, Private CHARLES
HOGG, Private THOMAS
McCANN, Private JOHN
McKAY, Private RICHARD
MADDEN, Private HENRY
PENMAN, Private ROBERT
WATERS, Corporal ALEXANDER

Royal Scots Fusiliers.

COLLINS, Private PATRICK
KERR, Private SAMUEL

Royal Warwicks.

TURNBULL, Private HENRY

Royal West Kents.

KELLY, Private JAMES
McDONALD, L/Corporal PETER
McVICOR, Private MICHAEL
SCOTT, Private THOMAS

Scots Guards.

MARSHALL, Private ANDREW
NICHOLSON, Private WILLIAM

Scottish Horse Field Ambulance.

NISBET, Private JOHN S.

Scottish Rifles.

McCURDIE, Private SAMUEL

Seaforth Highlanders.

BURNS, Private CHARLES
CAMERON, Private ROBERT
DYER, Private JOSEPH
JOHNSTONE, Private JOHN
KERR, Private ALLAN C.
MARTIN, Private WILLIAM
SMITH, Private THOMAS

H.M. Royal Navy and R.N.D.

BOYLE, Acting Leading Seaman JAMES, R.N.D.
BRYSON, Gun Layer LEWIS I.
LOCHHEAD, Able Seaman GORDON DRYNAN
McLOUGHLIN, Able Seaman FELIX
QUINN, Able Seaman WILLIAM

Australian Infantry Forces.

BOYLE, Private OWEN

Canadian Infantry.

CAMPBELL, Private ALEXANDER
M'LEAN, Private DANIEL SINCLAIR

Denny and Dunipace

Roll of Honour

The fallen men marked * left widows.

The decorated men marked † have received public presentations from the people of Denny and Dunipace in appreciation of the honour brought by them to the district.

ADAM, DANIEL, 84 Duke Street. A.M.I.E., R.A.F. No. 219329. Joined February 1915.

ADAM, DAVID, Broadyett. Able Seaman, R.N.D. No. R./2163. Joined August 1916.

ADAM, H. RUSSELL P., 44 Fankerton. Lieutenant, Scottish Rifles. * Joined September 1914.

ADAM, WILLIAM, 45 Glasgow Road. Private, 1st Cameron Hrs. No. 16693. Joined January 1915.

AINSLIE, JAMES, 26 Milton Row. Private 7th Cameron Hrs. No. 220230. Joined November 1916.

AITKENHEAD, ABRAHAM, West Borland Road. Private, A. & S. Hrs. Joined 1915.

ALEXANDER, CHARLES, 3 Anderson Street. Private, 7th A. & S. Hrs. No. 275975. Joined November 1914.

ALLAN, JAMES, 36 Fankerton. L/Corporal, Gordon Hrs. No. 7271. Joined November 1914.

ALLAN, JOHN, 4 Rosebank Court. Private, K.O.S.B. No. 17726. Joined January 1915.

ALLAN, JOHN, 41 Herbertshire Street. Private, Royal Scots Fusiliers. No. 53274. Joined June 1918.

ALLAN, JOHN, 36 Fankerton. Private, Gordon Hrs. No. 15337. Joined August 1916.

ALLAN, THOMAS R., Greenbank Cottage. Signaller L/Corporal, Black Watch. No. 350304. Joined November 1914. *Killed in action.*

B

STIRLING STREET, DENNY.

ALLAN, WILLIAM, 4 Rosebank Court. Private, Seaforth ·Hrs.
No. 655257. Joined June 1918.

ALLISON, ALLAN, 23 Broad Street. Private, K.O.S.B. *Killed in action.*

ANDERSON, ALEXANDER R., Dryburgh. Petty Officer, E.R.A.
No. 160302. Joined August 1918.

ANDERSON, DAVID, Lochlea. Private, Grenadier Guards. No.
23287. Joined March 1915. *Killed in action.*

*ANDERSON, GEORGE, 10 West Borland Road. Private, Royal
Scots. No. 38249. Joined October 1916. *Killed in action.*

†ANDERSON, JOHN, 127 Duke Street. Q.-M. Sergt., 8th Batt.
Royal Hrs. No. 41549. Joined November 1903. *Distinguished Conduct Medal.*

ANDERSON, ROBERT G., 13 Stirling Street. .Lieutenant, King's
Royal Rifles. Joined August 1914.

ANDERSON, ROBERT, Dryburgh. Sapper, R.E. No. 400578.
Joined November 1915.

ANDERSON, THOMAS, 61 Stirling Street. Private, Dorsets.
No. 12767. Joined January 1915.

ANDERSON, WILLIAM, Union Terrace. Sapper, Motor Cyclist
Co. R.E. No. 288546. Joined November 1915.

ANDERSON, WILLIAM, 14 West Borland Road. Air Mechanic,
R.F.C. No. 116665. Joined 1917.

ANDREW, ANDREW F., Annickvale. Gunner, R.F.A. No. 239428.
Joined February 1916.

ANDREW, GEORGE H., Annickvale. L/Corporal, A.S.C. No.
S/255356. Joined December 1916.

ANDREW, JOHN M'D., Annickvale. A.C.2, R.A.F. No. 268144.
Joined July 1918.

ANDREW, ROBERT, Annickvale. Sergt., H.L.I. No. 240989.
Joined May 1915.

ANDREW, WILLIAM M., Annickvale. Corporal, A.S.C. No.
235609. Joined September 1916.

ARNOTT, HENRY, 2 Fankerton. Pioneer, R.O.D., R.E. No.
W.R./288806. Joined June 1916.

ASHWOOD, WILLIAM, 202 Stirling Street. Bombardier, R.G.A.
No. 26354. Joined February 1907. *Killed in action.*

Those can conquer who believe they can.

VIRGIL

BAILLIE, JAMES, 154 Stirling Street. Private, Cameron Hrs. No. 33258. Joined 1918.

BAILLIE, WILLIAM, 154 Stirling Street. Gunner, R.G.A. No. 30074. Joined 1915.

BAIN, ROBERT J., Broompark U.F. Manse. Chaplain (Captain). Joined November 1917.

BAIN, WILLIAM A., Broompark. Private, A. & S. Hrs. No. 19466. Joined 1917.

BAIRD, J., Milton Row. Private, A. & S. Hrs.

BAIRD, JONATHAN, East Borland Square. Sergt., A. & S. Hrs. No. 1481. Joined 1915. *Killed in action.*

BAIRD, THOMAS, 58 Milton Row. Sapper, R.E. No. 156386. Joined November 1914.

BAIRD, WILLIAM J., 195 Stirling Street. L/Corporal, A. & S. Hrs. No. 6469. Joined November 1914. *Died of wounds.*

BALDWIN, JAMES B., Heatherdale. Flight Cadet, R.A.F. Joined February 1918.

BALDWIN, JOHN C., Heatherdale. Regimental Sergt.-Major, A. & S. Hrs. Joined November 1914.

BALDWIN, WILLIAM R., Heatherdale. Corporal, 9th Royal Hrs. No. 238545. Joined February 1916.

BARR, ROBERT, 55 Milton Row. Private, 6th Dorsets. No. 12765. Joined January 1915.

BARRETT, PATRICK, Anchor View. Corporal, Black Watch. No. 13942. Joined October 1914.

BAXTER, HUGH G., 24 Duke Street. Corporal, Gordon Hrs. No. 8533. Joined January 1915.

BAXTER, JAMES J. G., 24 Duke Street. Private, Gordon Hrs. No. 5645. Joined September 1914.

BAXTER, JOHN, 12 Duke Street. Sapper, R.E. No. 322926. Joined June 1917.

BAXTER, WILLIAM, 22 Milton Row. Private, 7th A. & S. Hrs. Joined June 1915. *Died in hospital in Scotland after discharge.*

BAYNE, ALLAN, 19 Glasgow Road. Sapper, R.E. No. 326418. Joined May 1918.

BAYNE, JOHN, 19 Glasgow Road. Lieutenant, 124th Siege Battery, R.G.A. Joined April 1916.

DUNIPACE PARISH CHURCH.

BECK, HEZEKIAH, 20 Broad Street. Private, 4th A. & S. Hrs. No. 9232. Joined September 1914.

BEDFORD, THOMAS F., 139 Broad Street. Private, 1/7 Gordon Hrs. No. 19850. Joined May 1917. *Killed in action.*

BELL, JOHN T., Burnside Cottages. Private, 3/1 Lovat Scouts. Joined 1915.

BELL, WILLIAM, Grangeview, Denny. Corporal, R.G.A. No. 182392. Joined September 1917.

BELL, W. G., Dunipace House. M. Sergt.-Major, M.T.R., R.S.C. No. M/2046140. Joined January 1915.

BENNIE, CHARLES, 6 Bridgend Place. Signaller, 11th A. & S. Hrs. No. 19091. Joined February 1917. *Died of wounds.*

BEVERIDGE, ALEXANDER, 24 Broad Street. Private, 10th A. & S. Hrs. No. 22342. Joined September 1917.

BINNIE, JAMES, 36 Milton Row. Private, Ross Mountain Battery, R.G.A. Joined 1915.

†BLACK, ADAM, 88 Stirling Street. Corporal, 7th A. & S. Hrs. No. 275883. Joined November 1914. *Distinguished Conduct Medal.*

BLACK, ALEXANDER, 16 East Borland Place. Private, H.L.I. No. 12028. Joined Regular Army 1912. *Killed in action.*

BLACK, JOHN R., 88 Stirling Street. Private, Gordon Hrs. No. 30700. Joined June 1918.

BLACK, MOSES, 16 East Borland Place. Private, 9th Gordon Hrs. No. 5755. Joined September 1914.

BLAIKIE, JAMES, Stoneywood. Private, 1st A. & S. Hrs. No. 9683. Joined February 1905. *Killed in action.*

BLAIKIE, WILLIAM, 77A Union Terrace. Sergt., A. & S. Hrs. No. 7652. Joined September 1914.

BLAINE, BERTRAM, 68 Duke Street. Driver, R.F.A. No. 187686. Joined September 1916.

BLAIR, JAMES, 75A Milton Row. Private, H.L.I. No. 43301. Joined 1915. *Killed in action.*

BOATH, DAVID, Glasgow Road.

BOYCE, ANDREW, Stirling Street. Private, R.E. Joined 1916.

BOYCE, PATRICK J., Davies Row. Private, H.L.I. No. 202149. Joined 1916.

BOYCE, WILLIAM, 197 Stirling Street. Private, Scots Greys. Joined August 1914.

Speak less than thou knowest.
Motto of Denny Parish Council.

BOYLE, CHARLES, 32 Glasgow Road.

BOYLE, JAMES, 27 Herbertshire Street. A.L.S., R.N.D., "Drake." No. C2/5862. Joined 1915. *Died of wounds.*

BOYLE, OWEN, 27 Herbertshire Street. Private, Australian I.F. No. 369. Joined 1914. *Killed in action.*

BRACELIN, WILLIAM, Kilbirnie Close. Private, Glasgow Imperial Yeomanry. No. 1499. Reservist.

BRADBURY, JOSEPH, 25 Fankerton. Private, Gordon Hrs. No. 30172. Joined May 1918.

BRADBURY, THOMAS S., 25 Fankerton. Private, R.G.A. No. 135431. Joined December 1916.

BROCK, GEORGE F., 2 Dryburgh Terrace. Private, A. & S. Hrs. No. 202656. Joined February 1917. *Killed in action.*

BRODIE, DANIEL, 125 Duke Street. Sapper, R.E. No. 418370. Joined August 1915.

BRODIE, JAMES, 29 Fankerton. Private, Gordon Hrs. No. 7148 Joined November 1914. *Killed in action.*

BRODIE, JOHN, 193 Stirling Street. Private, 7th Company, R.A.M.C. No. 138562. Joined March 1917.

BRODIE, ROBERT, 29 Fankerton. Private, A. & S. Hrs. No. 28384. Joined April 1918.

*BROPHY, WILLIAM, 1 Fankerton. Driver, A.S.C. No. 295. Joined September 1914. *Died in hospital.*

BROWN, ABRAHAM, 23 Herbertshire Street. Corporal, Gordon Hrs. No. 6800. Joined November 1914. *Killed in action.*

BROWN, DAVID, 54 Broad Street. Private, Scots Guards. No. 12503. Joined December 1914.

BROWN, DAVID, 138 Stirling Street. Ordinary Seaman, H.M.S. "Vivid." No. 88907. Joined May 1918.

BROWN, JAMES, Broad Street. Private, R.E. No. 208370. Joined November 1916.

BROWN, J. B., Aitkenhead Cottage. Private, 1st A. & S. Hrs. No. 2940. Joined September 1914.

BROWN, W. E. G., Thorndale. Private, 2nd Gordon Hrs. No. 203016. Joined January 1917.

BRYSON, JOHN K., 113 Stirling Street. L/Corporal, 1/7th A. & S. Hrs. No. 1564. Joined March 1912.

DENNY AND DUNIPACE COTTAGE HOSPITAL.

BRYSON, JOSEPH K., 113 Stirling Street. Private, Seaforth Hrs.
No. 28796. Joined July 1918.

BRYSON, LEWIS I., 113 Stirling Street. Armourer's Crew, Royal
Navy. No. 15654. Joined June 1915. *Killed in action.*

BUCHANAN, ARCHIBALD, 177 Stirling Street. Gunner, R.F.A.
No. 660665. Joined May 1915.

BUCHANAN, JAMES, 177 Stirling Street. Able Seaman, R.N.D.
No. 7765. Joined November 1916. *Prisoner of war in
Germany.*

BULLOCH, JAMES W., Campbellfield. Private, Labour Corps.
No. 148579. Joined November 1915.

BULLOCH, THOMAS, 38 Milton Row. Private, Labour Corps.
No. 473423. Joined June 1916.

BULLOCH, WILLIAM, The Cross, Denny. Private, 1/8th A. & S.
Hrs. No. 20812. Joined May 1917.

BURNIE, WILLIAM, 214 Stirling Street. Private, K.O.S.B. Joined
September 1914.

BURNS, CHARLES, 63 Milton Cottage. Private, Seaforth Hrs.
No. 40591. Joined September 1914. *Killed in action.*

BURNS, DUNDONALD, 63 Milton Cottage. Private, 1st Gordon
Hrs. No. 44812. Joined April 1918.

BURNS, JAMES, 63 Milton Cottage. Private, Tyneside Scottish.
No. 325562. Joined October 1915.

BURNS, RICHARD, 7 Davies Row. L/Corporal, 2/9th Durham
L.I. No. 80057. Joined November 1914.

BUSBY, DUNCAN McN., Tygetshaugh. L/Corporal, 24th Batt.
Northumberland Fusiliers. No. 42360. Joined November
1915. *Killed in action.*

BUSBY, JOHN, 38 Milton Row. Private, 8th Royal Hrs. No.
401277. Joined April 1917.

BUSBY, JOHN, 185a Stirling Street. Private, Black Watch. No.
5673. Joined September 1914.

CAMERON, ALEXANDER, 70 Broad Street. Sergt., 7th A. & S.
Hrs. No. 1575. Joined August 1914.

CAMERON, JOHN, 90 Stirling Street. Private, R.A.S.C. No.
405865. Joined September 1914.

That which is not for the interest of the whole swarm is not for the interest of a single bee.   MARCUS AURELIUS.

CAMERON, ROBERT, 70 Broad Street. Private, 8th Seaforth Hrs. No. 10485. Joined January 1915. *Killed in action.*

CAMPBELL, ALEXANDER, 58 Glasgow Road. Private, 31st Canadians. No. 446372. Joined April 1915. *Died in hospital of wounds.*

CAMPBELL, JAMES, 28 Fankerton. Private, R.A.M.C. No. 7507. Joined January 1914.

CAMPBELL, JAMES M., Union Terrace. Private, Seaforth Hrs. No. 41836. Joined September 1917.

CAMPBELL, JOHN, 13 Stirling Street. Private, Gordon Hrs. No. 6799. Joined November 1914.

CAMPBELL, ROBERT, 139 Duke Street. Private, 7th A. & S. Hrs. No. 278130. Joined September 1916.

CAMPBELL, WILLIAM JOHN, Parish Council Chambers. Sergt., 3rd Canadian Field Ambulance. No. 33307. Joined August 1914. *Military Medal.*

CANNON, WILLIAM, 20 Broad Street. Private, Machine Gun Corps. No. 66316. Joined July 1916. *Died after discharge.*

CARRUTHERS, ROBERT, Nicholswalls Farm. Private, Royal Hrs. No. 292607.

CHALMERS, ALEXANDER C., Wellstrand. Private, H.L.I. Joined 1915.

CHALMERS, WILLIAM, 3 East Borland Place. Private, Royal Hrs. No. 350306. Joined November 1914.

CHAPMAN, HARRY, Milton Cottage. Shoeing Smith, R.F.A. No. 7914. Joined August 1914.

CHRISTIE, W. W., Stirling Street. Private, A. & S. Hrs. No. 262237. Joined March 1915.

CLARK, J. B., 40 Milton Row. Corporal, Manchesters. No. 62268. Joined 1911.

CLARK, ROBERT C., Schoolhouse. Lieut., 7th A. & S. Hrs. Joined May 1915.

CLEMENT, JAMES, 36 Stirling Street. Private, 7th A. & S. Hrs. No. 5758. Joined July 1916. *Killed in action.*

CLEMENT, PETER, 36 Stirling Street. Private, 11th A. & S. Hrs. No. 40300. Joined November 1914. *Killed in action.*

CLEMENT, THOMAS, 36 Stirling Street. Private, 14th Scottish Rifles. No. 1867. Joined March 1916.

DENNY ROMAN CATHOLIC CHURCH, ST ALEXANDER'S.

COLLINS, PATRICK, 20 Broad Street. Private, 2nd Batt. Royal Scots Fusiliers. No. 7798. Joined 1914. *Killed in action.*

†COLLYER, JOHN G., 139 Broad Street. Private, Gordon Hrs. No. 7112. Joined November 1914. *Military Medal.*

COLLYER, SAMUEL, 139 Broad Street. Private, Gordon Hrs. No. 17556. Joined March 1917.

COLMAN, JEREMIAH, 33 Broad Street. Private, Royal Dublin Fusiliers. No. 21272.

COMRIE, ANDREW, 264 Rosebank. Bombadier, R.F.A. No. 6531. Joined February 1915.

COMRIE, DANIEL, Stirling Street, Dunipace. Private, A. & S. Hrs. Reservist. *Prisoner of war in Germany.*

COMRIE, JAMES, 264 Stirling Street. Private, 1/7th Northumberland Fusiliers. No. 4064. Joined October 1914. *Killed in action.*

CONROY, THOMAS, 35 Herbertshire Street. Private, Leinster Regt. No. 3617. Joined 1914. *Killed in action.*

CONWAY, JOHN, 37 Broad Street. Private, Welsh Fusiliers. No. 78556. Joined July 1918.

COOK, ROBERT, 83 Stirling Street. Air Mechanic 2D, R.N.A.S. No. 19428. Joined 1916.

COUSLAND, JOHN, 16 Stirling Street. Sapper, R.E. No. 29119. Joined March 1917.

COUTTS, WILLIAM, 41A Glasgow Road. Private, Seaforth Hrs. No. 28117. Joined June 1918.

COYLE, BERNARD, 5 Herbertshire Street. Private, H.L.I. No. 20273. Joined June 1916.

COYLE, JAMES, 159 Wellstrand. Private, Royal Dublin Fusiliers. No. 30367. Joined June 1917. *Killed in action.*

COYLE, JOHN, 83 Duke Street. L/Corporal, 1/5th Gordon Hrs. No. 230030. Joined August 1914. *Killed.*

COYLE, JOSEPH, 83 Duke Street. Private, Machine Gun Corps. No. 29888. Joined September 1915. *Killed in action.*

COYLE, MICHAEL, Bridgend, Denny. Private, 3rd Royal Scots. No. 28706. Joined September 1914.

COYLE, PATRICK, 83 Duke Street. Corporal, 7th A. & S. Hrs. No. 275767. Joined September 1914.

This above all, to thine own self be true;
And it must follow, as the night the day,
Thou can'st not then be false to any man.

Hamlet.

COYLE, PETER, 83 Duke Street. Private, 10th A. & S. Hrs. No. 8673. Joined April 1915.

COYLE, WILLIAM, Hamilton Place. Private, A. & S. Hrs.

CRAFT, DAVID, 5 East Borland Square. Guardsman, 2nd Batt. Scots Guards. No. 13747. Joined March 1915.

CRAIG, HUGH, Duke Street. Gunner, R.F.A. No. 166925. Joined August 1916.

CRAMB, ALEXANDER S., Little Denny. Private, R.E. No. 126080. Joined August 1916.

CRAMB, JAMES, 13 East Borland. Private, Dorsets. No. 12820. Joined January 1915.

CRAWFORD, ARCHIBALD, 32 Milton Row. Sergt., 3rd Batt. Dorset Regiment. No. 8808. Joined January 1915.

*CRAWFORD, DAVID, 212 Stirling Street. Private, A. & S. Hrs. No. 275426. Joined August 1914. *Died of wounds.*

CRAWFORD, JOHN, 69 Milton Row. Private, 12th Batt. A. & S. Hrs. No. 4647. Joined September 1914.

CRAWFORD, JOHN, Herbertshire Street. Private, Oxford & Bucks. No. 12679. Joined August 1914.

CRAWFORD, WILLIAM, 5 Hamilton Place. L/Corporal, 1/9th G.H., H.L.I. No. 55894. Joined February 1917.

CROSSLEY, ABRAHAM, 108 Stirling Street. Private, 2nd Royal Dublin Fusiliers. No. 8929. Joined August 1914. *Prisoner of war in Germany.*

CROSSLEY, ANDREW, 17A West Borland Road. Private, Labour Corps. No. 122781. Joined March 1917.

CROSSLEY, THOMAS, 150 Stirling Street. Private, K.O.S.B. No. 16917. Joined November 1914.

CUMMING, GEORGE, Headswood Cottage. Corporal, Royal Hrs. No. S/7032. Joined December 1914. *Died of wounds.*

CUMMING, JOHN, 145 Broad Street. Private, Gordon Hrs. No. 292315. Joined December 1915.

CUNNINGHAM, JAMES, 195 Stirling Street. L/Corporal, 1st Gordon Hrs. No. 5215. Joined September 1914. *Killed in action.*

CUNNINGHAM, JOHN, 195 Stirling Street. L/Corporal, 12th Batt. A. & S. Hrs. No. 2470. Joined August 1914. *Killed in action.*

c

DENNY PUBLIC SCHOOL.

CUNNINGHAM, WILLIAM, 11 East Borland. Air Mechanic, R.A.F. No. 44908. Joined August 1916.

CURRAN, DENIS, 20 Broad Street. Private, Royal Dublin Fusiliers. *Killed in action.*

DAVIDSON, JOHN A., Stoneywood. Private, M.T., A.S.C. No. 18904. Joined June 1916.

DAVIES, EVAN, Aitkenhead Cottage. Private, A. & S. Hrs. No. 6626. Joined November 1914.

DAWSON, JAMES, 74 Broad Street. Bombardier, R.G.A. No. 42179. Joined August 1914.

DAWSON, JOHN, 74 Broad Street. Private, A. & S. Hrs. No. 5913. Joined September 1914. *Killed.*

DAWSON, WILLIAM, 74 Broad Street. Able Seaman, R.N.D. No. C.Z./4445. Joined May 1919. *Prisoner of war in Germany.*

DAWSON, WILLIAM, Dunipace Home Farm. Private, Royal Scots. No. 31195. Joined May 1916. *Prisoner of war.*

DEAS, WILLIAM, 5 Broad Street. Private, M.T., A.S.C. No. 175690. Joined December 1915.

DEGNEY, JAMES, 7 Rosebank. Private, 1st A. & S. Hrs. No. 7413. Joined August 1914.

DELANEY, JAMES, 3 Vennel, Broad Street. Private, A. & S. Hrs. No. 6319. Joined September 1914.

DELANEY, JAMES, Union Terrace. Sapper, R.E. No. 126430. Joined December 1915.

†DENHOLM, GEORGE, 9 Fankerton. L/Corporal, R.E. No. 107727. Joined October 1915. *Military Medal.*

DEVINE, FRANCIS, 208 Stirling Street. Private, 7th A. & S. H. No. 34360. Joined October 1914.

DEWAR, JAMES, 177 Stirling Street. Driver, Ross Mountain Battery, R.G.A. No. 5117. Joined November 1915.

DEWAR, JOHN, 177 Stirling Street. Private, Black Watch. No. 5804. Joined September 1914.

DEWAR, WILLIAM M., 177 Stirling Street. L/Corporal, 6th Cameron Hrs. No. 220055. Joined April 1917. *Died of wounds.*

This happy breed of men, this little world,
This precious stone set in the silver sea,
This land of such dear souls, this dear, dear land.

Richard II.

DICKSON, DAVID R., 42 Broad Street. L/Corporal, 7th A. & S. Hrs. No. 275466. Joined August 1914.

DICKSON, JAMES G., 42 Broad Street. Private, 4th Batt. Australian Infantry. No. 1184. Joined August 1914.

DOCHERTY, DENIS, Tygetshaugh. Private, A. & S. Hrs. No. 28287. Joined July 1918.

DON, WALTER, 38 Glasgow Road. Gunner, R.F.A. No. 142804. Joined January 1916.

DONALDSON, DAVID, 34 Fankerton. Private, 8/10th Batt. Gordon Hrs. No. 7110. Joined November 1914. *Killed in action.*

DONALDSON, EDWIN, 45 Glasgow Road. Private, 1st Camerons. No. 16694. Joined January 1915.

DONALDSON, JAMES, 34 Broad Street. Private, 9th Gordon Hrs. No. 12502. Joined July 1915. *Killed in action.*

DONALDSON, JOHN, Helenslea, Stoneywood. Private, H.L.I. No. 43291. Joined November 1914.

DONALDSON, JOHN CUMMING, Stoneywood. R.Q.-M. Sergt., Durham Light Infantry. No. 100605. Joined June 1915.

DOUGAL, WILLIAM, 163 Wellstrand. Able Seaman, "Hawke" Batt., R.N.D. No. C.Z./7303. Joined November 1915.

DOUGLAS, FINLAY, 47 Milton Row. Private, Gordon Hrs. No. 30734. Joined June 1918.

DOUGLAS, JAMES, 47 Milton Row. Private, 7th A. & S. Hrs. No. 1754. Joined September 1914.

DOUGLAS, JOHN, 47 Milton Row. Private, 1st A. & S. Hrs. No. 6937. Joined September 1914.

DRUMMOND, GEORGE, 6 Dryburgh Terrace. Sergt., 2nd Batt. A. & S. Hrs. No. 9613. Joined September 1914.

DRUMMOND, JOHN, Brewsterburn Cottage. Gunner, R.G.A. No. 144974. Joined March 1916.

DRYSDALE, JAMES, Fankerton. Private, A. & S. Hrs. *Killed.*

DRYSDALE, WILLIAM, Junior, Church Place. Private, Scottish Horse. No. 3659. Joined 1914.

DUCKENFIELD, JOSEPH, Crummocksteps. Private, 7th A. & S. Hrs. No. 1300. Joined August 1914.

†DUCKENFIELD, W. W., Crummocksteps. Sapper, R.E. No. 127580. *Military Medal and Bar.*

NO. I MACHINE, CARRONGROVE.

(Carrongrove Paper Co., Ltd.)

DUNCAN, JOHN F., 119 Duke Street. Guardsman, Scots Guards. No. 13048. Joined January 1915.

DUNCAN, ROBERT, Church Place. Private, 7th A. & S. Hrs. No. 40507. Joined November 1914.

*DUNION, JAMES, 3 Kilbirnie Close. L/Corporal, Northumberland Fusiliers. No. 42372. Joined November 1915. *Killed in action.*

DUNLOP, ANDREW H., 10 Church Place. M.T., A.S.C. No. 155809. Joined February 1916.

DUNN, ALEXANDER, 145 Stirling Street. Gunner, R.G.A. No. 144921. Joined November 1915.

DUNN, WILLIAM, 145 Stirling Street. Private, T. 1/7 A. & S. Hrs. No. 1567. Joined April 1912.

DUNNIGAN, JAMES, 7 Park Place. Private, 1/8th A. & S. Hrs. No. 303216. Joined March 1915. *Killed in action.*

DURHAM, WILLIAM, Stirling Street. Private, A. & S. Hrs. No. 485. *Killed in action.*

DYER, ALEXANDER F., 12 Dryburgh Terrace. Private, H.C.B. No. 3365. Joined November 1914.

DYER, HUGH, 12 Dryburgh Terrace. Private, Machine Gun Corps. No. 83757. Joined November 1916.

DYER, JOSEPH, 214 Stirling Street. Signaller, Machine Gun Corps. No. 87190. Joined December 1916.

DYER, JOSEPH, 26 Herbertshire Street. Private, Seaforth Hrs. No. 40892. Joined 1915. *Killed in action.*

DYER, PETER F., 12 Dryburgh Terrace. Private, Seaforth Hrs. No. 655520. Joined June 1918.

EARL, JAMES, Lilybank. Gunner, R.F.A. No. 218029. Joined February 1917.

EASTON, ALEXANDER, Church Lane, Dunipace. Sergt. 1/7th A. & S. Hrs. No. 1228. Joined August 1914.

EASTON, JAMES McC., 161 Hamilton Place. Private, M.G.C. No. 43301. Joined December 1916. *Killed in action.*

ERSKINE, JOHN, 158 Stirling Street. Private, Cameron Hrs. No 23178. Joined November 1915.

FAGAN, JOSEPH, 23 Broad Street. Sergt., 2nd Scottish Rifles. No. 40847. Joined January 1915.

Breathes there the man with soul so dead
Who never to himself hath said
This is my own, my native land.

SIR WALTER SCOTT.

FARQUHARSON, ALEXANDER, 110 Stirling Street. Private, A.S.C. No. T/4043062. Joined January 1915.

FARQUHARSON, JAMES, 26 Herbertshire Street. Corporal, Gordon Hrs. No. 7250. Joined November 1914.

*FERGUS, JAMES B., Stoneywood. Private, Royal Hrs. No. 202722. Joined June 1917. *Killed in action.*

FERGUS, WILLIAM E., 31 Stirling Street. Private, A. & S. Hrs. No. 202917. Joined November 1915.

FERGUSON, JAMES, Star Hotel. Sapper, 61st Company R.E. No. 276496. December 1915.

†FERGUSON, JOHN, Anchor Cottage, Dunipace. Private, 7th A. & S. Hrs. No. 275267. Joined April 1913. *Military Medal.*

FERGUSON, PETER, Saltpans. Private, M.G.C. No. 30024 Joined June 1915.

FERGUSON, PHILIP, Anchor Cottage, Dunipace. Gunner, R.G.A. No. 207551. Joined April 1918.

FERGUSON, ROBERT, Poppletrees. Sergt., Canadian Expeditionary Force. No. 105847. Joined December 1915.

FERGUSON, ROBERT, 66 Broad Street. Private, A.V.C. No. 1938. Joined December 1914.

FERGUSON, WILLIAM, Lochridge. Corporal, Machine Gun Corps. No. 108621. Joined April 1917.

FERGUSON, WILLIAM, Poppletrees. Private, 6th Seaforth Hrs. No. 285389. Joined April 1917.

FERRARI, GUIDO, 25 Broad Street. Private, H.L.I. No. 67736. Joined August 1918.

FINLAY, JOHN, East Borland Square. Private, Machine Gun Corps. No. 6233. Joined July 1915.

FINLAY, LAURENCE, East Borland Square. Gunner, R.G.A. No. 182997. Joined September 1917.

FISHER, ALEXANDER, 37 Fankerton. Able Seaman, Royal Navy. No. J/82265. Joined December 1917.

FLEMING, JOHN, Grangeview. Sergt., Cameron Hrs. No. 15759. Joined November 1914. *Meritorious Service Medal.*

FLEMING, WILLIAM, Blaefaulds. Private, 4th Cavalry Field Ambulance. No. 3870. Reservist.

DENNY PARISH CHURCH.
The Cross.

FORBES, ALEXANDER, 67 Stirling Street. L/Corporal, Seaforth
Hrs. No. 27362. Joined May 1918.

FORBES, ALEXANDER C., Police Station. L/Corporal, Gordon
Hrs. No. 10226. Joined 1915. *Killed in action.*

FORBES, JOHN, 179 Stirling Street. Motor Mechanic, R.N.M.B.R.
Joined February 1918.

FORBES, ROBERT S., 67 Stirling Street. Private, 1/1st H.C. Batt.
No. 24786. Joined April 1918.

*FORFAR, JAMES, 54 Milton Row. Private, 1st Cameron Hrs.
No. 6380. Reservist. *Killed in action.*

FORSYTH, ALEXANDER, 203 Stirling Street. Gunner, R.G.A.
No. 203700. Joined February 1918.

FORSYTH, ALEXANDER, 41 Milton Row. Private, 2nd A. & S.
Hrs. No. 26548. Joined June 1918.

FORSYTH, ARCHIBALD, 41 Milton Row. Private, K.O.S.B.
No. 17727. Joined January 1915.

FORSYTH, DAVID, Stripeside. Private, A. & S. Hrs. Joined
1915.

FORSYTH, GEORGE, Stoneywood. Private, A. & S. Hrs. No.
1645. Joined August 1914. *Prisoner of war in Germany.*

FORSYTH, JAMES, Kilbirnie Close. Private, 2nd A. & S. Hrs.
No. 6380. Reservist. *Prisoner of war in Germany.*

FORSYTH, JOHN W., 7 Lairox Terrace. Private, 7th A. & S.
Hrs. No. 1752. Joined August 1914.

FORSYTH, RALPH, Stripeside. Private, 8th Batt., Tank Corps.
No. 305223. Joined January 1915.

FOSTER, ALEXANDER, 83 Broad Street. Private, A. & S. Hrs.
No. 4897. Joined September 1914.

FOTHERINGHAM, GEORGE, Hamilton Place. Private, A. & S.
Hrs. No. 4744. Joined 1915.

FOTHERINGHAM J., 1 Hamilton Place. L/Corporal, 10th A. &
S. Hrs. No. 1881. Joined August 1914.

FRANCE, DANIEL, 33 Milton Row. Private, Royal Hrs. No.
203551. Joined September 1914.

FRANCE, GEORGE, 33 Milton Row. Private, 1st Royal Scots.
No. 10183. Joined December 1907.

FRANCE, JOHN, 33 Milton Row. Private, 12th Royal Scots
Fusiliers. No. 1455. Joined September 1914.

The moving finger writes, and having writ
Moves on ; nor all thy piety nor wit
Shall lure it back to cancel half a line,
Nor all thy tears wash out a word of it.

OMAR KHAYYAM.

*FRASER, JAMES, 2 Duke Street. Private, 3rd Royal Scots. No. 1915. Joined 1914. *Killed in action.*

FULTON, ANDREW, 29 Stirling Street. Gunner, R.G.A. No. 120739. Joined December 1915.

GALLACHER, PATRICK, 20 Broad Street. Private, Labour Corps. No. 479065.

GARDNER, FREDERICK, 119 Stirling Street. Private, Royal Scots Fusiliers. No. 52842. Joined May 1918.

GARDNER, ROBERT, 119 Stirling Street. Gunner, R.G.A. No. 129291. Joined November 1916.

GARDNER, WILLIAM, 119 Stirling Street. Gunner, R.G.A. No. 300738. Joined November 1915.

GARDNER, WILLIAM, 3A Hall Street. Private, Royal Scots. No. 35385. Joined May 1918.

GAULD, ALFRED, 40 Broad Street. L/Corporal, 2nd Black Watch. No. 13239. Joined August 1914.

GAULD, JAMES B., 31 Fankerton. Private, 10th A. & S. Hrs. No. 2651.

GAULD, JOHN GILLESPIE, 14 Milton Row. Private, A. & S. Hrs. No. 2650. Joined August 1914.

GAULD, WILLIAM M., 19 Fankerton. Sergt., Gordon Hrs. No. 7111. Joined November 1914.

GEMMELL, DAVID, 91 Broad Street. Private, H.C. Batt. Joined 1914.

GEMMELL, WILLIAM, 91 Broad Street. Private, A. & S. Hrs. No. 13324. Joined 1914.

GENTLEMAN, JAMES, 49 Stirling Street. Sapper, R.E. No. 340878. Joined October 1917.

GENTLEMAN, JOHN, 56 Broad Street. L/Corporal, Cameron Hrs. No. 41555. Joined January 1918.

GIBSON, A., 91 Broad Street. 3rd Scottish Pro. Batt. No. 3372. Joined 1915.

GIBSON, WILLIAM, School Cottage. Corporal, Black Watch. No. 350294. Joined September 1914.

GILFILLAN, ALEXANDER, 145 Stirling Street. Sapper, R.E. Signals. No. 418204. Joined November 1914.

THE CEMETERY, DENNY.

GILFILLAN, JOHN, 145 Stirling Street. Signaller, 1st Somerset L.I. No. 204450. Joined November 1915.

GILLAN, THOMAS, 6 Kilbirnie Close. Private, Scottish Rifles. No. 24552. Joined November 1915.

GILLESPIE, ALEXANDER, 12 Broad Street. Private, 6th Scottish Rifles. No. 2326. Joined 1914.

GILLESPIE, FULTON, Junr., 65 Herbertshire Street. Private, Royal Scots. No. 62768. Joined May 1918.

*GILLESPIE, ROBERT, 150 Stirling Street. Sapper, R.E. No. 186183. Joined January 1916. *Killed in action.*

GILLESPIE, ROBERT, Myothill. Private, A. & S. Hrs. No. 18578. Joined 1917.

GILLESPIE, THOMAS, 11 Hamilton Place. Gunner, R.G.A. No. 182900. Joined October 1916.

*GILLESPIE, WILLIAM, 49 Milton Row. Private, Gordon Hrs. No. 7488. Joined 1914. *Killed in action.*

GILLESPIE, WILLIAM, 11 Hamilton Place. Private, 7th A. & S. Hrs. No. 1453. Joined 1914.

GILLESPIE, WILLIAM H., Church House. Private, 7th A. & S. Hrs. No. 276570. Joined October 1915. *Died on Service.*

GILMOUR, ALEXANDER, Denovan Lodge. Orderly, Red Cross. Joined October 1918.

GILMOUR, GEORGE, 57 Stirling Street. Private, 12th A. & S. Hrs. Joined September 1914.

GOODSIR, ALEXANDER, Fankerton. Private, 10th A. & S. Hrs. No. 1599. Joined August 1914.

GOODSIR, JAMES B., 189 Stirling Street. Sergt., 10th A. & S. Hrs. No. 2734. Joined August 1914.

GORRIE, BENJAMIN, 93 Broad Street. Sergt., 1st Black Watch. No. 6715. Joined November 1914.

GORRIE, JAMES, 93 Broad Street. Private, 5th Dragoon Guards. No. 22065. Joined February 1916.

GORRIE, JOHN L., 62 Broad Street. Private, 2/2nd Lovat Scouts. No. 5290. Joined September 1914.

*GORRIE, THOMAS AND., 63 Milton Row. Corporal, 76th Labour Corps. No. 45172. Joined November 1915. *Died shortly after discharge.*

Not a day passes over the earth but men and women of no note do great deeds, speak great words, and suffer noble sorrows.

CHARLES READE, *The Cloister and the Hearth.*

GORRIE, WILLIAM, 93 Broad Street. Private, Royal Dublin Fusiliers. No. 28478. Joined September 1914.

GOSS, ROBERT, Stoneywood. Driver, R.A.S.C. No. 182. Joined September 1914.

GRAHAM, RICHARD, Duke Street, Denny. Private, Gordon Hrs. No. 41072. Joined July 1915.

GRAHAM, ROBERT, Denovan Mains. Private, 4th A. & S. Hrs. No. 25836. Joined May 1918.

GRANT, ALEXANDER, 1 East Borland Square. Private, 3rd A. & S. Hrs. No. 24431. Joined February 1917.

GRANT, ARTHUR, 1 East Borland Square. Private, Machine Gun Corps. No. 6235. Joined 1916. *Killed in action.*

GRANT, GEORGE, 7 East Borland Place. Private, A. & S. Hrs. No. 23273. Joined September 1917.

GRANT, HUGH, 25 Broad Street. Corporal, A. & S. Hrs. No. 275770. Joined September 1914.

GRANT, HUGH, 1 East Borland Square. Private, 12th A. & S. Hrs. No. 5836. Joined October 1914.

GRANT, HUGH, 112 Stirling Street. Private, 5th Reserve Cavalry Reg. Joined 1914.

GRANT, HUGH, 105 Stirling Street. Private, 1st Gordon Hrs. No. 21193. Joined February 1917.

GRANT, THOMAS, 105 Stirling Street. Private, A. & S. Hrs. No. 12201. Joined July 1915.

GRAY, MATTHEW H., 100 Broad Street. Private, Gordon Hrs. No. 43113. Joined February 1916.

GRAY, SCOTT, 100 Broad Street. Private, A. & S. Hrs. No. 275135. Joined August 1914.

GRAY, WILLIAM A., 100 Broad Street. Private, Royal Hrs. No. 7984. Joined January 1915. *Died of wounds.*

GRAY, WILLIAM, 18 Church Place. Private, 3rd Batt. A. & S. Hrs. No. 29150. Joined August 1918.

GREEN, GEORGE, 262 Stirling Street. Private, 9th Royal Scots. No. 62712. Joined May 1918.

GREENOAK, JAMES, Braemoray, Denny. 2nd Air Craftsman, R.A.F. No. 278082. Joined July 1918.

GREIG, WILLIAM McK., Kellyside, Denny. Sergt., Army Ordnance Corps. No. 09635. Joined September 1915.

D

DUNIPACE UNITED FREE CHURCH.

GRIBBON, MICHAEL, Milton Row, Dunipace. Private, Scottish
Horse. No. 153333. Joined 1917.

GUNN, ALEXANDER McL., Herbertshire Street. Private, Gordon
Hrs. No. 3801. Joined 1914.

GUNN, DAVID T., 13 Herbertshire Street. Private, Cameron Hrs.
No. 9155. Joined 1917.

GUNN, SYDNEY, 1 Park Place. Private, Essex Regiment.
No. 12962. Joined September 1914.

HAGEN, GEORGE, 43 Herbertshire Street. Private, 2nd K.O.S.B.
No. 22120. Joined September 1914.

HAIR, JOHN C., 26 Milton Row. Private, 10th Batt. Gordon
Hrs. Joined November 1914.

HAIR, ROBERT, 26 Milton Row. Private, A. & S. Hrs.
No. 19495. Joined March 1917.

*HALKETT, DAVID W., 7 Fankerton. Private, Coldstream Guards.
No. 18521. Joined July 1915. *Killed in action.*

HALL, JAMES G., 76 Duke Street. Private, 2nd A. & S. Hrs.
No. 14857. Joined November 1915.

HAMILTON, JAMES, Northfield. Private, R.F.A. Joined
November 1915.

HAMILTON, JOHN, 24 Broad Street. L/Corporal, Royal Engineers.
No. 155911. Joined January 1915.

HAMILTON, THOMAS, Northfield. L/Corporal, R.A.S.C.
No. 025785. Joined November 1914.

HAMMOND, HUGH, 42 Herbertshire Street. Private, A. & S. Hrs.
No. 26044. Joined May 1918.

HANNAY, PETER, Denovan Cottage. Private, 1st Black Watch.
No. 9214. Joined May 1915. *Died of wounds.*

HANNAY, THOMAS, Denovan Cottage. Orderly, Red Cross.
No. 15211. Joined December 1917.

*HARRIS, HARRY, 38 Broad Street. Private, 2nd H.L.I. No. 353051.
Joined June 1916. *Killed in action.*

HATTRICK, JOHN, Grangeview, Denny. Corporal, R.E.
No. 282310. Joined May 1917.

HAUGH, JAMES C., Union Terrace. Private, Scottish Horse.
No. 28105. Joined November 1915.

Never strike sail to a fear.

EMERSON, *Heroism.*

HAY, ALEXANDER, Comelybank. Corporal, 7th A. & S. Hrs. No. 1231. Joined August 1914.

HAY, JOHN, Comelybank. Driver, R.E. No. 163128. Joined May 1916.

HEENAN, JAMES, 20 Broad Street. Private, A. & S. Hrs. No. 9402. Joined September 1914.

HEENAN, JOHN, 4 Hamilton Place. Private, A. & S. Hrs. No. 9748. Joined October 1914.

HEENAN, LAURENCE, 19 Herbertshire Street. Private, A. & S. Hrs. No. 6222. Joined 1914. *Killed in action.*

HEENAN, PETER (PETER HENDRY), Broad Street. Private, 6th Div. Amm. Col. No. 7026. Joined September 1914.

HEENAN, THOMAS, Broad Street. Private, R.F.A. Joined 1914.

HENDERSON, GEORGE, 6 Fankerton. C.Q.-M. Sergt., H.L.I. No. 63786. Joined August 1914.

HENDERSON, JAMES, 28A Herbertshire Street. Private, R.A.M.C. No. 115385. Joined April 1917.

HENDERSON, JOHN, 28A Herbertshire Street. Bombardier, R.F.A. No. L/10554. Joined May 1915.

HENDERSON, JOHN, 197 Stirling Street. Private, Royal Scots. No. 21697. Joined August 1914.

HENDERSON, JOHN D., 37 Herbertshire Street. Gunner, R.G.A. No. 190536. Joined November 1916.

HENDERSON, THOMAS L., 4 Broad Street. Private, R.A.M.C. No. 81591. Joined November 1915.

HENDRY, ALEXANDER, Greenbank Cottage. Private, 1/7 A. & S. Hrs. No. 1568. Joined August 1914.

†HENDRY, ALEXANDER, Garth Cottage, Castlerankine. L/Corporal, A. & S. Hrs. No. 275133. Joined August 1914. *Military Medal.*

HENDRY, JAMES, 141 Duke Street. Private, Q.O.R.W. Kents. No. 4576. Joined October 1914.

HENDRY, JOHN, 143 Broad Street. Private, 10th A. & S. Hrs. No. 7174. Joined August 1914.

HEPBURN, JAMES, Carronbank, Denny. Private, R.A.S.C. No. S.4/044630. Joined January 1915.

HEPBURN, WILLIAM, Stoneywood Park, Denny. Able Seaman, R.N.V. Reserve. No. C.Z./8120. Joined July 1916.

ST PATRICK'S R.C. SCHOOL, DENNY.

HERD, WALKER, 30 Broad Street. Sergt., A. & S. Hrs.
No. 275939. Joined November 1914.

*HERMISTON, CHARLES, Stoneywood, Denny. Private, Royal
Scots. No. 34893. Joined September 1916. *Killed in
action.*

HERMISTON, JAMES, Junr., Stoneywood, Denny. Corporal,
Royal Scots Fusiliers. No. 13880. Joined September 1914.

HICKIE, JOHN (*alias* JOHN WILSON), Broad Street.

HIGGINS, JAMES JOSEPH, 13a West Borland Road. Driver,
Canadian Artillery. No. C/41154. Joined August 1914.

HIGGINS, JOHN, 13 West Borland Road. Private, 5th Cameron
Hrs. No. 16703. Joined December 1914. *Killed in
action.*

HIGGINS, WILLIAM, 13a West Borland Road. Private, 1st A. & S.
Hrs. No. 7116. Joined August 1914.

*HILLHOUSE, ROBERT, 78 Broad Street. Sergt., Machine Gun
Corps. No. 2258. Joined August 1915. *Killed in
action.*

HOGG, ADAM, 208 Stirling Street. Private, Labour Corps.
No. 462067. Joined October 1918.

HOGG, THOMAS, Carronvale, Dunipace. Private, 13th Royal Scots.
No. 26853. Joined October 1915. *Killed in action.*

HOWIE, JOHN, Burnside Cottages. Red Cross Attendant, Royal
Navy. No. M/18873. Joined February 1916.

HOWIE, WILLIAM, Burnside Cottages. L/Corporal, British Red
Cross Society. Joined August 1917.

HUME, JOHN, 115 Broad Street. Private, Lanarkshire Yeomanry.
No. 1971. Joined 1916.

HUME, THOMAS, 115 Broad Street. E/A. H.M.S. "Vermon."
No. M/130999. Joined 1918.

HUNTER, DAVID, 5 West Borland Road. Private, Air Force.
No. 197347. Joined June 1918.

HUNTER, JOHN F., Mount Pleasant, Denny. 2nd/A.M., Royal
Air Force. No. 88255. Joined December 1915.

HUNTER, MALCOLM, 127 Stirling Street. Private, Gordon Hrs.
No. 25069. Joined June 1918.

HUNTER, ROBERT, 127 Stirling Street. Private, Gordon Hrs.
No. 7206. Joined November 1914.

Love thou thy land, with love far brought
   From out the storied Past, and used
   Within the Present, but transfused
Thro' future time by power of thought.

LORD TENNYSON.

HUNTER, ROBERT, 45 Glasgow Road. L/Corporal, 3rd Royal Scots. No. 30155. Joined November 1915.

HUNTER, ROBERT R., 11 Park Place. Private, 1/6 Seaforth Hrs. No. 28510.

INGLIS, ADAM, 61 Stirling Street. Private, A. & S. Hrs.

JARVIS, ANDREW, 131 Duke Street. Private, R.A.M.C. No. 43484. Joined October 1914.

JENKINS, ARCHIBALD J., Woodside, Denny. Lieutenant, 23 Peshawar Mountain Battery, F.E., M.G.A. Joined February 1916.

JENKINS, DAVID B., Woodside, Denny. Able Seaman, R.N.V. Reserve. No. C/Z. 8107. Joined June 1916.

JENKINS, WILLIAM, 27 Duke Street. Private, 10th A. & S. Hrs. No. 9203. Joined May 1915.

JOHNSTON, ADAM D., Stoneywood, Denny. L/Corporal, R.E. No. 37145. Joined May 1915.

JOHNSTON, ALEXANDER P., 83 Stirling Street. Private, 2nd K.O.S.B. No. 28667. Joined December 1915.

JOHNSTONE, DONALD, 134 Stirling Street. Private, Gordon Hrs. No. 3976. Joined September 1914.

†JOHNSTONE, JAMES, 12 Stirling Street. Sergt., Royal Scots. No. 250751. Joined December 1914. *Military Medal.*

JOHNSTONE, JAMES, Union Terrace. S.B. Res., R.C. Hospital Ship. No. 719. Joined February 1916.

JOHNSTONE, JAMES, Mid Burnego. Private, A. & S. Hrs. No. 18486. Joined January 1917.

JOHNSTONE, JOHN, 48 Milton Row. Private, Seaforth Hrs. No. 21489. Joined January 1917. *Killed in action.*

JONES, WILLIAM E., 72 Glasgow Road. C.Q.-M. Sergt., Scottish Rifles. No. 36129. Joined July 1916.

KANE, EDWARD, Bridgend, Denny. Sergt., Royal Dublin Fusiliers. No. 19806. Joined April 1915.

KANE, FRANK, 1A Hall Street. Private, K.O.S.B. No. 16885. Joined November 1914.

WOODYETT PIT.

(Robert Addie & Sons' Collieries, Ltd.).

KANE, THOMAS, 158 Stirling Street. Private, 1st Royal Dragoons. No. 13630. Joined 1914.

KAY, ALEXANDER, 14 Church Place, Dunipace. Private, Lancaster Yeomanry. No. 14264. Joined 1917.

KAY, ALEXANDER G., Wellbank, Denny. Sapper, R.E. No. 934. Joined September 1915.

KAY, GEORGE L. R., 24 Fankerton. Private, M.G.C. No. 66769. Joined August 1915. *Prisoner of war in Germany.*

KAY, JAMES G., Wellbank, Denny. Sapper, R.E. No. 29213. Joined February 1917.

KAY, JOHN C., 24 Fankerton. Private, 6th Seaforth Hrs. No. 28509. Joined June 1918.

KAY, JOHN F., Wellbank, Denny. Driver, R.F.A. No. 6561. Joined February 1915. *Died of wounds.*

†KAY, ROBERT, 33 Fankerton. Gunner, R.F.A. No. 218104. Joined March 1917. *Military Medal.*

KAY, WILLIAM, 24 Fankerton. Sergt., R.A.F. No. 145431. Joined July 1915.

KEDDIE, JAMES, 2 Rosebank, Dunipace. Corporal, A. & S. Hrs. Joined 1914.

KEDDIE, JOHN, 2 Rosebank, Dunipace. Private, 8th Seaforth Hrs. No. 40900. Joined December 1914.

KEDDIE, THOMAS, 2 Rosebank, Dunipace. Private, 7th A. & S. Hrs. No. 275422. Joined March 1914.

KEDDIE, WILLIAM, Rosebank, Dunipace. Private, A. & S. Hrs. *Killed in action.*

KEEGAN, WILLIAM J., 42 Stirling Street. Private, 4th A. & S. Hrs. No. 25975. Joined May 1918.

KELLY, EDWARD, 10 Hamilton Place. Able Seaman, R.N. No. C/Z. 8859. Joined May 1917.

KELLY, HUGH, 6 Milton Row, Dunipace. Able Seaman, R.N. No. 56389. Joined August 1916.

KELLY, JAMES, 6 Milton Row, Dunipace. Private, Royal West Kents. No. 5332. Joined January 1915. *Killed in action.*

KELLY, JOHN, 208 Stirling Street. Gunner, R.G.A. No. 300741. Joined November 1915.

KELLY, JOSEPH, 15 West Borland Road. Driver, R.S.C. No. 61369. Joined 1915.

. . . . , thou hast not sav'd one drop of blood
In this hot trial.   *King John.*

†KELLY, THOMAS, 6 Milton Row. Private, M.G.C. No. 57296. Joined July 1916. *Military Medal.*

KELLY, THOMAS P., 10 Hamilton Place. Gunner, R.G.A. No. 207554. Joined January 1916.

KELLY, WILLIAM, 6 Milton Row. Private, A. & S. Hrs. No. 9003. Joined August 1914.

KELLY, WILLIAM, Stoneywood, Denny. Private, 1/8 Scottish Rifles. No. 203072. Joined July 1916.

KELLY, WILLIAM, Anchor Cottage. Private, Royal Scots Fusiliers. No. 60812. Joined June 1918.

KEMP, PETER, Quarter Mill. Private, 1st Cameron Hrs. No. 20610. Joined August 1915.

KENNEDY, DAVID, 77 Union Terrace. Private, 1st K.O.S.B. No. 47495. Joined December 1915.

KENNEDY, JAMES, 8 Duke Street. Private, 4th Seaforth Hrs. No. 28024. Joined June 1918.

KERR, ALEXANDER H., 135 Stirling Street. R.S.-M., 2nd A. & S. Hrs. No. 7078. Joined October 1899.

KERR, ALLAN C., Viewforth, Denny. Private, 8th Seaforth Hrs. No. 21651. Joined December 1916. *Killed in action.*

KERR, ANDREW A., 135 Stirling Street. Sergt., 7th A. & S. Hrs. No. 1917. Joined 1907. *Killed in action.*

KERR, GEORGE R., 135 Stirling Street. Private, 1st A. & S. Hrs. No. 1227. Joined July 1913. *Died at Salonica.*

KERR, JAMES, 17 West Borland Road. L/Corporal, 18th A. & S. Hrs. No. 9234. Joined May 1915.

KERR, JAMES, 135 Stirling Street. Sergt., R.A.M.C. No. 59245. Joined May 1915.

KERR, JAMES, 30 Milton Row. Private, Labour Corps. No. 312935. Joined July 1917.

KERR, JOHN, 17 West Borland Road. Private, A.O.C. No. 025786. Joined December 1916.

KERR, ROBERT, 5A Milton Row. Sergt., A.V.C. No. 218. Joined November 1915.

KERR, SAMUEL, 24 Milton Row. Private, Royal Scots Fusiliers. No. 16317. Joined January 1915. *Killed in action.*

KERR, THOMAS, Athole Place. Private, A. & S. Hrs. No. 28335. Joined July 1918.

DENNY PARISH COUNCIL OFFICES.

KERR, THOMAS H., 135 Stirling Street.   Private, 11th A. & S. Hrs.   No. S/40455.   Joined 1916.   *Killed in action.*

KERR, WILLIAM, Stoneywood, Denny.   Private, R.A.M.C.   No. 43491.   Joined October 1914.

KERR, WILLIAM, 17 West Borland Road.   Private, 5th A. & S.Hrs. No. 202126.   Joined December 1916.

KERR, WILLIAM G., 81 Stirling Street.   Pioneer, R.E. (Signal Service).   No. 341256.   Joined April 1917.

KING, WILLIAM, 122 Stirling Street.   Private, R.E.   No. 288054. Joined October 1914.

KIRKWOOD, ARCHIBALD, 127 Stirling Street.   Sergt., Canadian. No. 29110.   Joined September 1914.

KIRKWOOD, WILLIAM, 127 Stirling Street.   Sergt., 10th A. & S. Hrs.   No. 2934.   Joined September 1914.

LAIDLAW, JAMES, 44 Springfield Road.   Private, Gordon Hrs. No. 17372.   Joined December 1916.

LAIRD, CHARLES, Union Terrace.   Deckhand, H.M. M.-L. 555 Dover.   No. D.A/13337.   Joined September 1916.

LAIRD, HENRY, 1 Kilbirnie Close.   Private. 4th Seaforth Hrs. No. 28519.   Joined May 1918.

LAIRD, IRA GRENALL, 11 Herbertshire Street.   Signaller. R.N.D. Reserve.   No. 5458.   Joined June 1915.

LAIRD, WILLIAM, 87 Union Terrace.   2nd Lieutenant, H.L.I. Joined February 1915.

†*LAMBERT, CHARLES GRAHAM, Rosehill, Denny.   Gunner, R.F.A.   No. 192452.   Joined November 1916.   *Killed in action.   Military Medal.*

LAURIE, JOHN LESLIE, 83 Stirling Street.   Private, Royal Scots. No. 62777.   Joined May 1918.

LAW, DAVID, 26 Fankerton.   L/Corporal, 4/5 Royal Hrs.   No. 292853.   Joined June 1916.

LAW, THOMAS W., 18 Duke Street.

LAWRENCE, JAMES, Fankerton.   Private, N. Staffs.   Joined September 1914.   *Killed.*

LAWRIE, JAMES, 51 Herbertshire Street.   Private, R.A.M.C. No. 1906.   Joined 1915.

For God and the people.

Motto of Denny and Dunipace Town Council.

LAWRIE, JOHN, 7 Milton Row, Dunipace.   Corporal, Black Watch. No. 44101. Joined June 1918.

LAWSON, WILLIAM W., 49a Milton Row. Royal Hrs. No. 5993. Joined 1916.

LEA, GEORGE, Dryburgh, Denny. Cameron Hrs.

LENATHAN, JOHN, 9 Dryburgh Terrace. Private, 4th Reserve, Seaforth Hrs. No. S/26875. Joined April 1918.

†LENATHAN, PATRICK, 9 Dryburgh Terrace. Private, Royal Dublin Fusiliers. No. 19812. Joined April 1915. *Military Medal.*

LENATHAN, TIMOTHY, 9 Dryburgh Terrace. Private, 2nd Royal Munster Fusiliers. No. 1901. Joined September 1914.

LEVACK, ROBERT, Dryburgh Terrace. Private, Scots Guards. No. 1968. Joined 1915.

LIDDELL, DONALD F., Viewfield House. Private, Gordon Hrs. No. 40952. Joined November 1914.

LIND, ROBERT NEIL, 18 Duke Street. Cadet, R.A.F. No. 180602. Joined July 1918.

LISTER, JAMES, 12 East Borland. Private, Gordon Hrs. No. 8153. Joined December 1914.

LIVINGSTONE, GEORGE, 56 Herbertshire Street.   3rd Air Mechanic, R.A.F. No. 306726. Joined October 1918.

LOCHHEAD, GORDON DRYNAN, Melita Cottage.   Able Seaman, R.N.D. No. 5366. Joined June 1915. *Prisoner of war in Germany. Killed.*

LOCHHEAD, ROBERT ALLAN, Melita Cottage. Staff-Sergt., R.F.A. No. 103310. Joined September 1914. *Killed in action.*

LOCHHEAD, WILLIAM G., Melita Cottage. Lieut., 4th Royal Scots Fusiliers. Joined March 1915.

LOCKHART, JOHN W., Davies Row. Private, Gordon Hrs. No. S/10382. Joined June 1915. *Killed in action.*

LOGAN, WALTER, 5 East Borland. Corporal, A. & S. Hrs. No. 275143. Joined August 1914.

LONEY, DAVID, Union Terrace. Private, 4th Seaforth Hrs. No. 28112. Joined May 1918.

LONEY, JAMES, 42a Herbertshire Street. Private, 5/6th Royal Scots. No. 62683. Joined May 1918.

E

HERBERTSHIRE CASTLE, DUNIPACE.

Destroyed by fire on 20th December 1914. The Castle, as it stood at the time of the fire, dated from 1557, but the original building was probably erected some centuries earlier.

LONEY, THOMAS, Union Terrace. Private, A. & S. Hrs. No. 279057. Joined September 1914.

LORIMER, ALEXANDER, Grangeview. Private, 7th A. & S. Hrs. No. 3380. Joined November 1914. *Died of wounds.*

LORIMER, ALFRED, Grangeview. Private, 8th Black Watch. No. 9190. Joined May 1915. *Died of wounds.*

LYNN, ALEXANDER, Gote Loan. Gordon Hrs. No. 3374. Joined November 1915.

LYNN, JAMES, 19 Herbertshire Street. Private, 4th Batt. A. & S. Hrs. No. 9714. Joined October 1914.

LYNN, JAMES, 81 Duke Street, Denny. Private, Royal Hrs. No. 4226. Joined September 1914.

LYNN, JOHN, 19 Herbertshire Street. Sapper, R.E. No. 601084. Joined July 1917.

MADDEN, HENRY, 50 Milton Row. Private, 17th Batt. Royal Scots. No. 25672. Joined June 1915. *Died in hospital (Scotland).*

MADDEN, HENRY, 103 Stirling Street. Private, R.E. No. 333416. Joined April 1918.

MADDEN, PATRICK, Broad Street. Private, Royal Welsh Fusiliers.

MARMARA, LEWIS, 6 West Borland Road. Naval Division, O.S.I. No. 363696. Joined 1916.

*MARSHALL, ANDREW, 54 Broad Street. Private, Scots Guards. No. 12502. Joined December 1914. *Died of wounds.*

MARSHALL, JOHN, 56 Milton Row. Private, Seaforth Hrs. and M.G.C. No. 192850. Joined August 1918.

MARSHALL, PETER, 50a Herbertshire Street. Private, 3rd Cameron Hrs. No. 33244. Joined July 1918.

MARSHALL, ROBERT, 96 Broad Street. Private, 10th P.W.O. Royal Hussars. No. 54206. Joined May 1918.

MARSHALL, ROBERT, 50a Herbertshire Street. Private, 7th Seaforth Hrs. No. 27361. Joined May 1918.

MARSHALL, WILLIAM, 23 Herbertshire Street. Private, Lovat Scouts. No. 464944. Joined March 1917. *Died in hospital.*

†MARTIN, SAMUEL, 198 Stirling Street. Private, 7th A. & S. Hrs. No. 275425. Joined March 1914. *Military Medal.*

Whoever fights, whoever falls,
Justice conquers evermore.

EMERSON, *Voluntaries.*

MARTIN, WILLIAM, 198 Stirling Street. Private, 8th Seaforth Hrs. No. 40904. Joined November 1914. *Killed in action.*

MEALLS, JOHN, 196 Stirling Street. Air Mechanic, R.A.F. No. 27584. Joined October 1914.

MEALLS, JOHN McM., 15A Milton Row. Private, 1st London Scottish. No. 516159. Joined January 1918.

MEALLS, WILLIAM K., 15A Milton Row. Private, H.L.I. No. 1930. Joined November 1914.

MELVIN, JOHN, 69 Duke Street. Private, Royal Munster Fusiliers. No. 1032. Joined September 1914.

MERCER, ALEXANDER R., Meadowbank. Lieut., Gurkha Rifles (Indian Army). Joined November 1915.

MERCER, JAMES, Meadowbank. Sergt., A. & S. Hrs. No. 7648. Joined September 1914.

MICHIE, ROBERT, 45 Grangeview. Private, Gordon Hrs. No. 10706. Joined April 1915.

MILLAR, JAMES, Denny Mill. Farrier, A.S.C. No. 7/S7935. Joined January 1915.

MILLAR, THOMAS, Denny Mill. Gunner, R.F.A. No. 187623. Joined October 1916.

†MILLER, ANDREW, Stirling Street. Sergt., A. & S. Hrs. No. 9306. Joined 1914. *D.C.M. Prisoner of war in Germany.*

MILLER, D., Stirling Street. Private, Royal Scots.

MILLER, JAMES, 10 Fankerton. Private, 1/7th Gordon Hrs. No. 22643. Joined August 1917. *Killed.*

MILLER, JAMES B., 11 Milton Row. Sergt., 7th A. & S. Hrs. No. 202205. Joined August 1914.

MILLER, JOHN, 2 Dryburgh Terrace. Private, Seaforth Hrs. No. S/27249. Joined May 1918.

MILLER, ROBERT, 37 Herbertshire Street. Sapper, T.W.D., R.E. No. 330795. Joined 1918.

MITCHELL, DAVID McC., 81 Stirling Street. Private, 5th A. & S. Hrs. No. 29894. Joined September 1918.

MITCHELL, GEORGE, 81 Stirling Street. Private, K.O.S.B. No. 222217. Joined January 1915.

*MITCHELL, JAMES H., 33 Herbertshire Street. Royal Scots, M.G.C. No. 83072. Joined November 1916. *Killed in action.*

BAPTIST CHURCH.

MITCHELL, JOHN, 81 Stirling Street. Private, K.O.S.B. No. 17604. Joined May 1915. *Killed in action.*

MITCHELL, JOHN A., 52 Herbertshire Street. Private, 6th D.L.I. No. 277299. Joined November 1915.

MITCHELL, SAMUEL, 81 Stirling Street. Sergt., K.O.S.B. No. 8654. Regular before War. *Killed in action.*

MITCHELL, WILLIAM McN., 81 Stirling Street. Private, K.O.S.B. No. 17604. Joined January 1915. *Killed in action.*

MOFFAT, JOHN, 12 Milton Row, Dunipace. Corporal, 7th A. & S. Hrs. No. 275894. Joined November 1914.

MOFFAT, JOHN, 18 Church Lane. Private, Naval Brigade, 16th Section. No. 304. Joined September 1914.

MOFFAT, JOSEPH, 12 Milton Row. Gunner, R.G.A. No. 207552. Joined April 1918.

MOFFAT, ROBERT, 61 Stirling Street. Sapper, R.E. No. 21250. Joined February 1911.

MOIR, WILLIAM, Tops, Denny. Private, 6th Batt. Royal Hrs. Joined June 1916.

MOONEY, DANIEL, Tygetshaugh, Dunipace. Private, R.E. No. 292467. Joined July 1915.

MOORE, GEORGE, 61 Stirling Street. Private, Army Ordnance Corps. No. 4559. Reservist.

MORRAN, GEORGE A., 87 Stirling Street. Private, 3rd Gordon Hrs. No. 6775. Reservist.

MORRISON, ALEXANDER, 155 Broad Street. Private, Seaforth Hrs. No. S/27197. Joined May 1918.

MORRISON, ANTHONY, 62 Broad Street. L/Corporal, A. & S. Hrs. No. 275465. Joined August 1914.

MORRISON, GEORGE, 155 Broad Street. Sapper, R.E. (Signals). No. 161319. Joined May 1916.

MORRISON, JAMES, 62 Broad Street. Private, London Scottish. No. 528144. Joined August 1914.

MORRISON, JAMES, 155 Broad Street. Corporal, Black Watch. No. 350295. Joined October 1914.

MORRISON, JAMES, 18 Duke Street. Private, Royal Scots. No. 34802. Joined September 1916.

MORRISON, JOHN, 62 Broad Street. Signaller, R.F.A. No. 68790. Joined January 1915.

Theirs not to make reply,
Theirs not to reason why,
Theirs but to do and die.

TENNYSON, *The Charge of the Light Brigade.*

MORRISON, THOMAS, 155 Broad Street. Corporal, R.E. No. 418258. Joined April 1915.

MORRISON, WILLIAM, 6 East Borland. Private, M.T., R.A.S.C. No. 020627. Joined November 1914.

MORRISON, WILLIAM, 89 Broad Street. Private, 7th A. & S. Hrs. No. 277572. Joined June 1916.

MUIR, ROBERT, 72 Duke Street. Private, 1/1st H.C.B. No. 350717. Joined August 1916.

MUIR, WILLIAM, 9A Hall Street. Private, H.L.I. No. 33156. Joined December 1917.

MULLAN, JOHN, Tygetshaugh, Dunipace. Private, Royal Scots. No. 62762. Joined May 1918.

MULLEN, JOHN, 91 Stirling Street. Rifleman, Royal Irish Rifles. No. 8780. Joined September 1915. *Died in hospital, Scotland.*

†MURDOCH, GEORGE, 18 Duke Street. Corporal, Gordon Hrs. No. 291134. Joined 1916. *Military Medal. Prisoner of war in Germany.*

MURPHY, ALEXANDER, Anchor House. Private, A. & S. Hrs. No. 4583. Joined September 1914.

MURPHY, PATRICK, Boghead Place. L/Corporal, Royal Munster Fusiliers. No. 3069. Joined September 1914. *Killed in action.*

MURPHY, PATRICK, 15 West Borland Road. Private, Royal Scots. No. 62691. Joined May 1918.

MURPHY, THOMAS, 15 West Borland Road. Private, A. & S. Hrs. No. 3639. Joined August 1914.

MURRAY, ADAIR D., 58A Herbertshire Street. Private, 9th Seaforth Hrs. No. 28111. Joined June 1918.

MURRAY, CHARLES, 125 Duke Street, Private, A. & S. Hrs. No. 104385. Joined June 1916.

MURRAY, GEORGE W., 58A Herbertshire Street. Private, 52nd H.L.I. No. 71839. Joined June 1918.

MURRAY, MICHAEL, 4 Duke Street. Private, 27th Batt. Northumberland Fusiliers. No. 42414. Joined October 1915. *Killed in action.*

MURRAY, ROBERT CLARK, 1 Fankerton. Private, R.E. (T.B.). No. 260169. Joined February 1917.

McANESPIE, WILLIAM, Grangeview. Corporal, R.A.S.C. No. 255855. Joined 1917.

DUNIPACE PUBLIC SCHOOL.

McARTHUR, ANDREW, 240 Stirling Street. Private, H.C.B.
No. 1659. Joined November 1914.

McARTHUR, GEORGE, 83 Broad Street. Driver, R.F.A. No.
239405. Joined November 1915.

McARTHUR, JAMES, 240 Stirling Street. Private, 1/7th A. &
S. Hrs. No. 2168. Joined August 1914. *Killed in action.*

McARTHUR, SAMUEL, Stirling Street. Private, A. & S. Hrs.

McARTHUR, WILLIAM, 83 Broad Street. L/Corporal, 8th A. &
S. Hrs. No. 13190. Joined August 1915.

McATEER, JAMES, 10 Kilbirnie Close. Able Seaman, R.N. No.
55821. Joined July 1916.

McATEER, JOHN, 10 Kilbirnie Close. Private, Royal Welsh
Fusiliers. No. 22215. Joined June 1915.

*McATEER, PATRICK, 29 Milton Row. Private, 2nd R.I. Rifles.
No. 7303. Reservist. *Killed in action.*

McBRYDE, DUNCAN. Private, A. & S. Hrs.

McBRYDE, JAMES, 108 Stirling Street. Private, 7th Seaforth
Highlanders. No. 28115. Joined June 1917.

McBRYDE, PETER, 108 Stirling Street. Private, 53rd Gordon
Hrs. No. 29881. Joined August 1917.

McCAFFERTY, JOHN, 12 Kilbirnie Close. Private, Royal Scots.
No. 23084. Joined May 1915.

McCAFFERTY, NEIL, 27 Herbertshire Street. Private, 3rd
Royal Dublin Fusiliers. No. 19805. Joined April 1915.

McCALLUM, JAMES, 46 Milton Row. Private, G.M.G. Corps,
No. 6901. Joined June 1918.

McCANDLISH, PATRICK DALMAHOY, Quarter House.
Brevet Lieut.-Colonel, A. & S. Hrs. Recalled to Colours
as Captain, August 1914. *C.B.E.* (*Military*). *D.S.O.*
White Eagle of Servia.

McCANN, JOHN, 5 Davies Row. Sapper, R.E. No. 298351.
Joined January 1915.

McCANN, JOHN, 37 Broad Street. Private, 2nd Royal Scots. No.
40421. Joined February 1916. *Killed in action.*

McCARTNEY, PATRICK, 103 Stirling Street. Private, Royal
Irish Rifles. Joined May 1915.

McCORMICK, JAMES L., 75 Union Terrace. Gunner, R.F.A.
No. 951542. Joined July 1915.

Dulce et decorum est pro patria mori.—HORACE.
(It is sweet and glorious to die for one's country.)

McCORMICK, JOSEPH, 75 Union Terrace. Private, Royal Irish Regiment. No. 26380. Joined July 1917.

McCORMICK, PETER, 13 Stirling Street. A. & S. Hrs. Joined April 1916.

McCORMICK, WILLIAM, 13 Stirling Street. O. Seaman, R.N.D. No. Z.C.6650. Joined 1915.

McCORMICK, WILLIAM, 170 Stirling Street. Private, Royal Scots. No. 62682. Joined May 1918.

McCROARY, JOHN, 16 Milton Row. Private, R.A.M.C. No. 54853. Joined January 1915.

McCULLOCH, JOHN, 29 Stirling Street. Private, Dublin Fusiliers. No. 19804. Joined April 1915. *Killed in action.*

McCURDIE, SAMUEL, 37 Broad Street. Private, Scottish Rifles. Joined August 1914. *Killed in action.*

McDONALD, ANGUS, 141 East Borland. Private, 50th Batt. M.G.C. No. 171076. Joined April 1918.

McDONALD, HENRY, Kilbirnie Close. Private, H.L.I. No. 64163. Joined July 1918.

†McDONALD, HUGH, Comely Bank. Corporal, R.E. No. 76102. Joined August 1914. *Military Service Medal.*

McDONALD, JOHN, 1 Rosebank Court. Private, 1st Batt. L. Regiment. No. 4108. Joined January 1915.

McDONALD, JOHN, 47 Broad Street. Wireman, R.N. No. M/25614. Joined June 1915.

†McDONALD, JOHN, Comely Bank. Lieutenant, 7th A. & S. Hrs. Joined May 1915. *Military Cross.*

McDONALD, KENNETH R. G., Comely Bank. Bombardier, R.F.A. No. 144230. Joined May 1916.

McDONALD, NORMAN D. A., Comely Bank. Bombardier, R.F.A. No. 175377. Joined August 1916.

McDONALD, PETER, Milton Row, Dunipace. L/Corporal, Royal West Kents. No. 5331. *Killed in action.*

McDONALD, WILLIAM, 52 Milton Row. Private, R.E. No. 79245. Joined September 1914.

McDONALD, WILLIAM, 141 East Borland. Private, 12th A. & S. Hrs. No. 130611. Joined September 1914.

McDONALD, WILLIAM, Stirling Street. Private, A. & S. Hrs.

PART OF MOULDING SHOP, DENNY IRON WORKS.
(Cruikshank & Co., Ltd.)

McDOUGALL, JOHN, Fankerton. Driver, A.S.C. Remounts. No. 111547. Joined June 1915.

McDOUGALL, PETER, Hallhouse, Denny. Sapper, 529th Field Co. R.E. No. 420419. Joined March 1916.

McEWAN, ALEXANDER, 62 Broad Street. Private, Scots Greys. Joined August 1914.

McEWAN, ALEXANDER E., Robelle, Dunipace. Signaller, A. & S. Hrs. No. S/7643. Joined September 1914. *Killed in action.*

McEWAN, EWAN, Robelle, Dunipace. Signaller, K.O.S.B. No. 32075. Joined November 1915.

McEWAN, HENRY, 5A Hall Street. Gunner, R.F.A. No. 167166. Joined August 1916.

McEWAN, JAMES, Robelle, Dunipace. Gunner, R.G.A. No. 300739. Joined November 1915.

McEWAN, NEIL, 5A Hall Street. L/Corporal, Cameron Hrs. No. 15850. Joined November 1914.

McEWAN, THOMAS, 100 Meadowbank. Private, Black Watch. No. 6705. Joined November 1914.

McEWAN, WILLIAM, 2 East Borland Square. Private, 12th H.L.I. No. 33. Joined September 1914.

McFARLANE, ANDREW, East Borland Square. Private, H.L.I. No. 18703. Joined September 1914.

McFARLANE, GEORGE, 46 Broad Street. 3rd A.M., R.A.F. No. 307423. Joined October 1918.

McFARLANE, JOHN A., 48 Herbertshire Street. Gunner, R.F.A. No. 175740. Joined December 1915.

McGARR, JAMES, 3 Star Close. Private, R.I. Rifles. No. 683876. Joined July 1918.

McGEACHIE, CHARLES, 9 Hall Street. Private, 6th Seaforth Hrs. No. 24011. Joined January 1917.

McGEACHIE, JOHN, 9 Hall Street. Private, 10th A. & S. Hrs. No. 40532. Joined April 1915. *Killed in action.*

McGEACHIE, JAMES, 152 Stirling Street. Private, R.W. Kents. No. 4413. Joined January 1915.

McGEE, JOHN, 33 Broad Street. Private, Labour Corps. No. 526178. Joined 1915.

Howe'er it be, it seems to me
'Tis only noble to be good.
Kind hearts are more than coronets,
And simple faith than Norman blood.
TENNYSON, *Lady Clara Vere de Vere.*

McGINLAY, JAMES, Herbertshire Street. Private, 1st Scots Guards. No. 6981. Reservist. *Prisoner of war in Germany.*

McGINLAY, MICHAEL, 8 East Borland Place. Private, 3rd Scottish Horse. No. 306. Joined August 1914.

McGINLAY, WILLIAM, 8 East Borland Place. Private, A. & S. Hrs. Joined August 1914.

McGLADE, JAMES, 83 Duke Street. Private, Royal Scots Greys. No. 9180. Joined September 1914.

McGLADE, JOHN, Tygetshaugh, Dunipace. C. Sergt.-Major, 11th A. & S. Hrs. No. 3630. Joined September 1914. *Killed in action.*

McGOVERN, HENRY, 6 Carron Terrace. L/Corporal, R. Irish Regiment. No. 18256. Joined January 1917.

McGREGOR, JOHN, Junior, 122 Stirling Street. L/Corporal H.L.I. No. 29663. Joined March 1917.

McGRORTY, PATRICK, 43 Milton Row. Private, Irish Guards. No. 7208. Joined March 1915. *Killed in action.*

McGRORY, JAMES, Springbank House. Bombardier, B. M. Battery. No. 300762. Joined February 1916.

McGUCKIN, EDWARD, 87 Stirling Street. Sapper, R.E. No. 145713. Joined April 1902. *Reservist.*

McGUIRE, FRANCIS, 5 Fankerton. Sergt., R.F.A. No. 6632. Joined December 1914.

McGUIRE, JAMES, 23 Broad Street. Private, 8th Royal West Kents. No. 4411. Joined January 1915.

McGURK, ARCHIBALD, 125 Duke Street. Driver, 52nd D. Sig. Co. No. 418385. Joined August 1915.

McGURK, JOSEPH, Stoneywood. Private, Royal Irish Rifles. No. 7199. Joined May 1915.

McHALE, JAMES, 126 Stirling Street. Private, M.T., R.A.S.C. No. 138727. Joined November 1915.

McINTYRE, JAMES A., 119 Stirling Street. Fitter Gunner, R.G.A. No. 142305. Joined May 1912.

McINTOSH, JOHN, 202 Stirling Street. Corporal, D.L.I. No. 200651. Joined November 1915.

McKAY, RICHARD R., 268 Stirling Street. Private, Royal Scots. No. 34811. Joined September 1916. *Died of wounds.*

DENNY WEST UNITED FREE CHURCH.

McKAY, THOMAS, 268 Stirling Street.   Private, Royal Scots.   No. 382086.   Joined September 1916.

McKENNA, ARDEL, Stoneywood House.   Private, A. & S. Hrs. No. 1751.   Joined August 1914.

McKENNA, FRANCIS, Stoneywood House.   Signalman, Royal Navy.   No. 5461.   Joined June 1915.

McKENNA, JAMES, Stoneywood House.   Rifleman, 2/16th London Regiment.   No. 245710.   Joined February 1918.

McKENNA, THOMAS P., Stoneywood House.   Private, M.G.C. No. 74044.   Joined February 1917.

McKENZIE, ALEXANDER, 18 Springfield Road.   Private, M.G.C.   No. 27289.   Joined November 1915.

McKENZIE, ALEXANDER, 137 Duke Street.   Cameron Hrs. Joined 1915.

McKENZIE, ARCHIBALD W., 15 Milton Row.   Private, 10th Gordon Hrs.   No. 7244.   Joined November 1914.   *Presumed killed.*

McKENZIE, GEORGE M., 146 Broad Street.   Private, 2nd Seaforth Hrs.   No. 40876.   Joined December 1914.

McKENZIE, HENRY T., 139 Broad Street.   Private, A. & S. Hrs. Joined August 1914.   *Killed in action.*

McKENZIE, JAMES T., 15 Milton Row.   Private, 1/6th Black Watch.   No. 268359.   Joined June 1916.

McKENZIE, JOHN, 146 Broad Street.   Private, M.T., R.A.S.C. No. 132670.   Joined October 1915.

MACKIE, ROBERT C., Fankerton, Denny.   Private, Gordon Hrs. No. 11093.   Joined 1914.   *Killed in action.*

McKILLOP, ROBERT, Carronvale.   Private, M.T., R.A.S.C.   No. 187858.   Joined June 1916.

McKINLAY, JOHN, 19 Milton Row.   Private, 7th A. & S. Hrs. No. 434020.   Joined July 1916.

McKINLAY, THOMAS, 40 Springfield Road.   L.S. R.N.V. Reserve "Clyde."   No. Z/3421.C.   Joined January 1915.

McLACHLAN, DONALD C., Glasgow Road.   Captain, R.A.M.C. Joined August 1915.

McLAREN, DANIEL, 69 Milton Row.   L/Corporal, A. & S. Hrs. No. 14044.   Joined November 1914.

McLAREN, DANIEL, 43 Fankerton.   Stoker, 1st Class, Royal Navy.   No. K/34535.   Joined November 1915.

Ring in the Valiant Man and free,
  The larger heart, the kindlier hand;
  Ring out the darkness of the land,
Ring in the Christ that is to be.

In Memoriam.

McLAREN, DANIEL, Helenslea, Dunipace. Private, L.S. Sharp-
shooters. No. 32048. Joined March 1917.

McLAUGHLIN, DANIEL, 60 Boghead Place. Private, Gordon
Hrs. No. 5663. Joined September 1914.

McLAUGHLIN, JOHN, 37 Broad Street. Private, Royal Irish
Fusiliers. Joined 1914.

McLEAN, DANIEL, 68 Broad Street. Private, 25th Bn. Canadians.
No. 415989. Enlisted 1915. *Killed in action.*

McLOUGHLIN, DANIEL, 9 Park Place. Private, A. & S. Hrs.
No. 2950. Joined September 1914.

McLOUGHLIN, FELIX, 9 Park Place. Able Seaman, R.N.D.
No. Z/5130. Joined June 1915. *Killed in action.*

McLUSKIE, JAMES, Stoneywood, Denny. Private, 10th Gordons.
No. 7113. Joined November 1914.

McMAHON, OWEN, 8 Milton Row, Dunipace. Private, A. & S.
Hrs. No. 29030. Joined August 1918.

McMENEMY, BERNARD, 18 Milton Row. Corporal, Royal West
Kents. No. 4860. Joined December 1914.

McMENEMY, PATRICK, 18 Milton Row. Driver R.F.A. No.
40824. Joined August 1914.

McMILLAN, DAVID, Dajena Villa. L/Corporal, 7th Gordons.
203001. Joined January 1916.

McMILLAN, JOHN, Dajena Villa. Driver, R.A.S.C. No.
T4/243022. Joined September 1914.

McMULLAN, JOHN, 66 Boghead Place. Petty Officer, R.N.D.,
D. Batt. No. 7271. Joined November 1915.

McMULLAN, JOHN D., 33 Broad Street. Gunner, R.F.A. No.
196361. Joined March 1916.

McMURDO, GAVIN, 44 Herbertshire Street. Private, Cameron
Hrs. No. 15440. Joined November 1914.

McMURDO, HUGH A., 62 Broad Street. Gunner, R.G.A. No.
301655. Joined November 1915.

MacMURDO, JOHN J., 23 Herbertshire Street. Gunner, R.F.A.
No. 646640. Joined September 1916.

†MacMURDO, ROBERT, 23 Herbertshire Street. Private, Cameron
Hrs. No. 15437. Joined November 1914. *Military Medal.*

MacMURDO, ROBERT, 187 Stirling Street. Private, Seaforth Hrs.
No. 28187. Joined June 1918.

BROOMPARK UNITED FREE CHURCH.

McMURDO, ROBERT S., 62 Broad Street. Private, Seaforth Hrs. No. 28186. Joined June 1918.

McMURDO, THOMAS S., 62 Broad Street. L/Corporal, D.L.I. No. 323030. Joined November 1915.

McNALLY, PATRICK, 22 Duke Street. Private, 3rd Royal Scots. No. 62682. Joined May 1918.

McNAUGHTON, JOSEPH, 16 Dryburgh Terrace. Private, 10th H.L.I. (S.B.). No. 43865. Joined June 1916.

McNEIL, JOSEPH, 42 Stirling Street. Private, A. & S. Hrs. No. 3198. Joined 1914. *Killed in action.*

McNEIL, PATRICK, 42 Stirling Street. Private, Gordon Hrs. No. 5537. Joined 1915. *Killed in action.*

McPHIE, CHARLES, 122 Stirling Street. L/Corporal, A. & S. Hrs. No. 6052. Joined Sept. 1914.

McPHIE, JOHN, 83 Union Terrace. L.A.C. R.A.F. No. 18189. Joined December 1915.

McQUADE, FRANCIS, 2 Park Place. Private, A. & S. Hrs. No. 27711. Joined June 1918.

McQUADE, HENRY, 2 Park Place. Corporal, Coldstream Guards. No. 22201. Joined February 1917.

McQUEEN, JOHN, Clydesdale Bank House. Private, R.A.M.C. No. 128519. Joined January 1918.

McQUEEN, ROBERT, 53 Milton Row. Private, R.E. No. 505953. October 1916.

McQUEEN, WILLIAM, 53 Milton Row. Private, H.L.I. No. 8128. Joined August 1914.

McVICOR, MICHAEL, 42 Milton Row, Dunipace. Private, Royal West Kents. No. 5333. Joined January 1915. *Killed.*

McWATT, JOHN S., 141 Stirling Street. Instructor, R.A.F. No. 266763. Joined July 1918.

†McWATT, WILLIAM, 64 Boghead Place. Coporal, 409th Field Co. R.E. No. 412488. Joined July 1915. *Military Medal.*

McWATT, WILLIAM, Marybank, Denny. Private, Gordon Hrs. No. 30815. Joined June 1918.

†NEIL, JOHN F., Park Place. 2nd Lieutenant, A. & S. Hrs. Joined 1913. *Military Medal.*

There is no Death! What seems so is transition.
  This life of mortal breath
Is but a suburb of the life elysian,
  Whose portal we call Death.

LONGFELLOW'S *Resignation*.

NEIL, THOMAS, Park Place. Corporal, 7th A. & S. Hrs. No. 275093. Joined January 1912.

NEILL, JOHN, 240 Stirling Street. Private, Seaforth Hrs. No. 28785. Joined July 1918.

NEILSON, ALEXANDER, 85 Stirling Street. Drummer, A. & S. Hrs. No. 1476. Joined August 1914. *Killed in action.*

NEILSON, JAMES, 85 Stirling Street. L/Corporal, Royal Munster Fusiliers. No. 1050. Joined September 1914. *Killed in action.*

†NEISH, ALEXANDER MILLAR, Viewfield Villas. 2nd Lieutenant, 7th A. & S. Hrs. Joined November 1914. *Died of wounds. Military Cross.*

NELSON, ANDREW, 143 Stripeside. Private, 7th Seaforth Hrs. No. 28113. Joined June 1918.

NELSON, JAMES, 143 Stripeside. Private, 7th A. & S. Hrs. No. 2466. Joined May 1915.

*NELSON, McLAREN JOHN, 16 Springfield Road. Private, A. & S. Hrs. No. 40616. Joined May 1916. *Drowned in Germany, 4th November* 1919.

NEWLANDS, ROBERT, Randolph Hill. Private, M.T., R.A.S.C. No. 183816. Joined May 1916.

NICHOLSON, CHARLES, Burnside Cottages. L/Corporal, A. & S. Hrs. No. 18206. Joined November 1916.

NICHOLSON, JAMES, Slafarquhar, Denny. Private, 3rd Batt. K.O.S.B. No. 25388. Joined June 1916.

NICHOLSON, WILLIAM, Slafarquhar, Denny. Private, Scots Guards. No. 11438. Joined October 1914. *Died of wounds.*

NISBET, ANDREW. Private, A. & S. Hrs.

NISBET, JAMES, Lynemore. Gunner, D/250 Bde. R.F.A. No. 916081. Joined December 1915.

NISBET, JOHN STEWART, Lynemore. Private, S.H. F. Ambulance. No. 92466. Joined July 1915. *Died in East Africa.*

NISBET, ROBERT, 144 Stirling Street. Private, Royal Air Force. No. 191742. Joined June 1918.

O'BOYLE, MICHAEL, Junr., 149 Stirling Street. Private, A. & S. Hrs. No. 26414. Joined June 1918.

TORWOOD CASTLE, DUNIPACE.

(In ruins.) Probably erected about 1565.

O'DONNEL, JAMES, 10 Park Place.   Private, Royal Dublin Fusiliers. No. 29275.   Joined January 1917.

O'DONNEL, JOHN, 112 Stirling Street.   Private, A. & S. Hrs. No. 4166.   Joined April 1915.

O'DONNELL, CHARLES, 14 East Borland.   Private, Royal Scots. No. 25671.   Joined June 1915.

O'DONNELL, HENRY, 14 East Borland.   Private, 3rd A. & S. Hrs. No. 26045.   Joined May 1918.

O'DONNELL, THOMAS, 133 Stirling Street.   Private, Royal Scots. No. 35387.   Joined June 1918.

O'HANLON, EDWARD, Dryburgh Terrace.   Private, Royal Munster Fusiliers.   No. 2957.   Joined 1915.   *Killed in action.*

O'HANLON, JOSEPH, 5 Park Place.   Able Seaman, R.N.V. Reserve. No. C. Z/6630.   Joined October 1915.

OLSEN, CHRISTIE, 22 Glasgow Road.   Private, M.T., R.A.S.C. No. 350641.   Joined October 1917.

O'ROURKE, JOSEPH, 266 Stirling Street.   Private, R.D. Corps. No. 7312.   Joined August 1914.

O'ROURKE, JOSEPH, Junr., 266 Stirling Street.   Private, Royal Scots.   No. 29476.   Joined October 1915.

O'ROURKE, MICHAEL, 266 Stirling Street.   Drummer, 3rd A. & S. Hrs.   No. 22488.   Joined July 1917.

PARK, JOHN, 230 Stirling Street.   L/Corporal, A. & S. Hrs. No. 1484.   Joined September 1914.   *Killed in action.*

PATERSON, ALEXANDER, 52 Broad Street.   Pioneer, R.E. No. 338850.   Joined August 1916.

PATERSON, DAVID D., Croftfoot, Dunipace.   L/Corporal, 2nd Gordon Hrs.   No. 12151.   Joined July 1915.   *Killed in action.*

PATERSON, GEORGE, 74 Duke Street.   Corporal, 7th A. & S. Hrs. No. 275085.   Joined August 1914.

PATERSON, GEORGE, 49 Herbertshire Street.   Pioneer, R.E. No. 51763.   Joined 1915.

PATERSON, HENRY, 60 Glasgow Road.   Private, Scots Guards. No. 12904.   Joined January 1915.

PATERSON, JAMES, 151 Stirling Street.   Private, Seaforth Hrs. No. 28110.   Joined 1918.

We live in deeds, not years; in thoughts, not breaths;
In feelings; not in figures on a dial.

Philip J. Bailey.

PATERSON, JOHN, 246 Stirling Street.   Sergt., 7th A. & S. Hrs. No. 58.   Joined August 1914.

†PATERSON, JOHN, East Borland Square.   Private, M.G.C. No. 89108.   Joined December 1916.   *Military Medal.*

PATERSON, JOHN F., 52 Broad Street.   Private, Scots Guards. No. 19465.   Joined February 1918.

PATERSON, JOHN H., Croftfoot, Dunipace.   Private, 10th A. & S. Hrs. No. 26528.   Joined June 1918.

PATERSON, ROBERT, Carronvale, Dunipace.   Sapper, R.E.   No. 94635.   Joined April 1915.

PATERSON, ROBERT, Old Quarter, Dunipace.   Private, M.G.C. No. 117390.   Joined February 1916.

PATERSON, SAMUEL, Old Quarter House.   Private, 3rd A. & S. Hrs. No. 390269.   Joined April 1917.

PATERSON, THOMAS, Milton Row, Dunipace.   Sergt., K.O.S.B. No. 6001.   Joined Regular Army before War.

PATERSON, WILLIAM, 87 Stirling Street.   Private, 2nd A. & S. Hrs. No. 6572.   Joined November 1914.

PATERSON, WILLIAM, Old Quarter House.   Private, 7th Royal West Kents.   No. 381050.   Joined September 1914.

PATRICK, ANDREW, Burnside Cottages.   Signalman, R.N.V. Reserve.   No. 7615.   Joined November 1915.

PATRICK, JAMES, Glasgow Road.   Able Seaman, Royal Navy. No. 206452.   Joined November 1914.

PATTERSON, JOHN R., 7 Hall Street.   L/Corporal, G.C.L.C. No. 234857.   Joined December 1916.

PAUL, DUNCAN S., 74 Broad Street.   Sapper, R.A.M.C.   No. W.R/279989.   Joined August 1915.

PAUL, GEORGE C., 27 Glasgow Road.   Private, 7th Cameron Hrs. No. 15851.   Joined November 1914.

PAUL, JAMES, Burnhouse Cottage.   Private, 10th A. & S. Hrs. No. 26529.   Joined June 1918.

PEACOCK, ALEXANDER R., East Borland.   Sergt., H.L.I. No. 1663.

PEAT, DAVID MEALLS, Stirling Street.   C.Q.-M. Sergt., Scottish Horse.   No. 153478.

PEDDIE, JOHN, 26 Milton Row.   L/Corporal, M.G.C.   No. 84444. Joined November 1916.

DENNY AND DUNIPACE WAR HEROES' MEMORIAL COMMITTEE.

Chairman—Provost John A. Lochhead, J.P. (middle figure of front row).

Joint Secretary—Alexander Hendry, Town Clerk (on Chairman's right).

Treasurer, Editor of Roll of Honour, and Joint Secretary—James Rankine, Clerk to Denny Parish Council (on Chairman's left).

PEEBLES, CHARLES W., 79 Union Terrace. Sergt., R.G.A. No. 345484. Joined April 1916.

PENMAN, JOHN, 60 Milton Row. Private, Royal Hrs. No. 2767. Joined March 1916.

PENMAN, ROBERT, 60 Milton Row. Private, Royal Scots. No. 30291. Joined March 1916. *Killed in action.*

PINKERTON, THOMAS, 34 Milton Row. Private, Seaforth Hrs. No. 28121. Joined June 1918.

*PLANNER, LEONARD, Quarter. Piper, 2nd A. & S. Hrs. No. 8151. Reservist. *Killed in action.*

PORTEOUS, JOHN, 23A Broad Street. Private, A. & S. Hrs. No. 6471. Joined November 1914.

PRESTON, JAMES, 61 Stirling Street. Private, R.A.M.C. No. 56860. Joined March 1915.

PRICE, GEORGE, 106 Stirling Street. Able Seaman, R.N.D. No. C/Z7301. Joined November 1915.

PRICE, GEORGE, 37 Broad Street. Private, A. & S. Hrs. No. 9653. Joined September 1914.

PRICE, PATRICK, 106 Stirling Street. Private, A. & S. Hrs. No. 26410. Joined May 1918.

PRINGLE, ALEXANDER, Annslea, Denny. Private, 11th Royal Hrs. No. 39181. Joined December 1915.

PRYDE, JOHN, 76 Stirling Street. Gunner, R.F.A. No. 227153. Joined April 1917.

PURVIS, JAMES, Denovan, Denny. Sergt., S.R., C.M.U. No. 3641. Joined June 1915.

QUIGLEY, JAMES, 10 Kilbirnie Close. Corporal, Royal Irish Rifles. No. 607811. Joined October 1915.

QUINN, WILLIAM, Milton Row. Able Seaman. Joined May 1914. *Drowned* 1914.

RAE, JAMES, Stoneywood. Sergt., A. & S. Hrs. No. 1641. Joined August 1914. *Missing.*

REID, ANDREW, 121 Duke Street. Private, M.T., R.A.S.C. No. 117826. Joined August 1915.

REID, JOHN, Duke Street. Private, 75th Batt. Canadian Infantry. No. 690862. Joined April 1916.

I have fought a good fight, I have finished my course, I have kept the faith. *English Bible*, 2 Tim. iv. 7.

REID, PETER, Duke Street. Private, 1st Batt. Canadian Infantry.
No. 407016. Joined May 1915. *Killed in action.*

REID, WALTER, 121 Duke Street. Bombardier, Royal Horse
Artillery. No. 113194. Joined October 1915.

REILLY, PATRICK, 5 Lairox Terrace. Private, Connaught Rangers.
No. 8201. Joined 1917.

RETSON, JAMES, 11 Herbertshire Street. Private, 2nd A. & S. Hrs.
No. 7114. Joined August 1914.

RETSON, JOHN, 28 Stirling Street. Driver, R.F.A. No. 646732.
Joined September 1916.

RETSON, ROBERT, 155 Broad Street. Private, 1/5 K.O.Y.L.I.
No. 201525. Joined November 1914.

ROBERTSON, ALEXANDER, 91 Broad Street. Private, Scots
Guards. No. 12903. Joined January 1915.

ROBERTSON, DAVID, Kirkslap. Private, A. & S. Hrs.

ROBERTSON, JOHN, Stoneywood. L/Corporal, 10th A. & S. Hrs.
No. 2534. Joined August 1914. *Missing, presumed killed.*

ROBERTSON, PETER, 91 Broad Street. Private, Royal Hrs.
No. 43053. Joined 1916.

ROBERTSON, ROBERT, 84 Duke Street. Private, R.A.M.C.
No. 13184. Joined August 1915.

ROBERTSON, THOMAS, 64 Broad Street. Sergt., 6th Royal Hrs.,
T.F. No. 162. Joined April 1908.

RYAN, PETER, 138 Stirling Street. Able Seaman, R.N.D.,
"Hawke" Batt. No. 5863. Joined August 1915.

*SCOBIE, JOHN McD., Stoneywood. Private, 1/7 Black Watch.
No. 6650. Joined June 1916. *Killed in action.*

SCOTT, ALBERT, 138 Stirling Street. Private, A. & S. Hrs.
No. 1752. Joined September 1914. *Killed in action.*

SCOTT, ALEXANDER, 37 Broad Street. Private, A. & S. Hrs.
No. 275787. Joined September 1914.

SCOTT, ALEXANDER, 3 Park Place. Private, 1st Gordon Hrs.
No. 1492. Joined August 1914.

SCOTT, CHARLES McK., 3 Park Place. Private, A Co., 29th
Batt. Canadian. No. 422925. Joined December 1915.

SCOTT, DAVID, 124 Stirling Street. Private, R.A.S.C. No. 425678.
Joined July 1915.

G

Go, and rest,
With heroes 'mid the Islands of the Blest,
Or in the fields of empyrean light.
A meteor wert thou in a darksome night.

WORDSWORTH.

SCOTT, DUNCAN, 158 Stirling Street. Private, 17th H.L.I. No. 43282. Joined October 1914.

SCOTT, GEORGE, 79A Milton Row. Private, A. & S. Hrs. No. 279234. Joined April 1915.

SCOTT, GEORGE, 22 Fankerton. Private, 1st L. N. Lancashires. No. 36058. Joined October 1916.

SCOTT, JAMES, Carronbridge. Private, H.L.I. No. 41576.

SCOTT, JAMES H., 102 Glasgow Road. Private, East Lancashire Reg. No. 33386. Joined 1915. *Killed in action.*

SCOTT, JAMES S., 3 Park Place. L/Corporal, R.E. No. 9466. Joined October 1915.

SCOTT, JOHN, 3 Park Place. Co. Sergt.-Major, 9th Batt. A.I.F. No. 3927. Joined November 1915.

SCOTT, JOHN, 158 Stirling Street. Private, Gordon Hrs. No. 27925. Joined June 1918.

SCOTT, JOHN, 100 Broad Street. Private, Labour Corps. No. 1668.

SCOTT, JOHN D., 8A Church Place. Private, 5th Cameron Hrs. No. 24267. Joined November 1915. *Prisoner of war in Germany.*

SCOTT, PETER, 2 Duke Street. Private, 4th Res. Seaforth Hrs. No. 25567. Joined September 1917.

SCOTT, THOMAS, 22 Fankerton. Private, 8th Royal West Kents. No. 5341. Joined January 1915. *Missing.*

SCOTT, WILLIAM, 11 Fankerton. Private, 1st A. & S. Hrs. No. 2536. Joined August 1914.

SCOTT, WILLIAM, 3 Park Place. Private, Black Watch. No. 350131. Joined 1915.

SHANKS, ALEXANDER, 195 Stirling Street. Corporal, R.F.A. No. 50224. Joined August 1914.

SHANKS, ALEXANDER, Broomhill, Denny. Private, 10th A. & S. Hrs. No. 26524. Joined June 1918.

SHANKS, DAVID, East Borland, Denny. Driver, M.T., R.A.S.C. No. 237188. Joined December 1914.

SHANKS, JOHN W., 18 Church Lane, Dunipace. R.N.D. No. A 304. Joined 1914.

SHANKS, ROBERT, 29 Duke Street. Private, A. & S. Hrs. No. 19248. Joined 1917.

How sleep the brave who sink to rest
By all their country's wishes blest!
When Spring, with dewy fingers cold,
Returns to deck their hallowed mould,
She there shall dress a sweeter sod
Than Fancy's feet have ever trod.

W. COLLINS.

SHANKS, WILLIAM, Broomhill, Denny. Gunner, R.F.A. No. 640773. Joined August 1917.

SHARP, JAMES, 149 East Borland. Private, 7th Batt. A. & S. Hrs. No. 1565. Joined August 1914. *Killed in action.*

SHARP, WILLIAM, 149 East Borland. Private, Gordon Hrs. No. 31405. Joined July 1918.

SHEARER, JOHN M., Kellyside, Denny. Private, 10th A. & S. Hrs. No. 7649. Joined September 1914.

SHEPHERD, WILLIAM, 89 Broad Street. Private, Royal West Kents. No. 4586. Joined November 1914.

SHERLOCK, THOMAS, 79 Milton Row, Dunipace. Private, A. & S. Hrs. No. 233403. Joined March 1917.

SHIRRA, WILLIAM, Herbertshire Street. Private, Seaforth Hrs. No. S/6350. Joined 1915.

SHORT, EDWARD, Broad Street. Private, H.L.I. No. 12713. Joined 1915.

SIMPSON, ALEXANDER, Duncarron Place. Private, 10th Scottish Rifles. No. 43603. Joined February 1916.

SIMPSON, JAMES, 49 Fankerton. Able Seaman, R.N.V. Reserve. No. C/Z. 8121. Joined July 1916.

SIMPSON, ROBERT, Duncarron Place. Private, 7th A. & S. Hrs. No. 40205. Joined 1914.

SIMPSON, WILLIAM, Gow's Buildings, Stoneywood. Corporal, Royal Scots Fusiliers. No. 16577. Joined January 1915.

SIMPSON, WILLIAM, 14 Hamilton Place. Private, 1/4 Gordon Hrs. No. 20372. Joined May 1917.

SINCLAIR, DONALD, 58 Herbertshire Street. Private, 50th Canadians. No. 435754. Joined September 1915.

SINCLAIR, EDWARD, 8 Kilbirnie Close.˙ Private, 1st Batt. H.L.I. No. 7440. ˙Joined 1914. *Killed in action.*

SINCLAIR, JAMES, 8 Carron Terrace. Private, 12th H.L.I. No. 18384. Joined 1915.

SINCLAIR, JOHN, 13 Herbertshire Street. Private, K.O.S.B. No. 16884. Joined November 1914.

SINCLAIR, JOHN, 68 Broad Street. Private, 2/7 A. & S. Hrs. No. 4117. Joined 1915.

SINCLAIR, JOHN, 90 Stirling Street. Private, 1st Bdg. Canadians. No. 11620. Joined August 1914.

One who never turned his back but marched breast forward.
  Never doubted clouds would break,
Never dreamed, though right were worsted, wrong would triumph,
Held we fall to rise, are baffled to fight better,
          Sleep to wake.   BROWNING.

SINCLAIR, MICHAEL, 68 Broad Street. Private, K.O.S.B. No. 5965. Joined May 1917.

SINCLAIR, ROBERT, 80 Stirling Street. Private, A. & S. Hrs. No. 9472. Joined September 1914.

SINCLAIR, ROBERT, 13 Herbertshire Street. Private, 2nd A. & S. Hrs. No. 26376. Joined May 1918.

SINCLAIR, WILLIAM McG., 58 Herbertshire Street. L/Corporal, M.T., R.A.S.C. No. 137160. Joined October 1915.

SKINNER, GEORGE, 23 Fankerton. Private, 3rd H.L.I. No. 54013. Joined April 1918.

SLOAN, WILLIAM, 149 Stirling Street. Private, K.O.S.B. No. 29230. Joined August 1914.

SMALL, HUGH, Nethermains. Private, Gordon Hrs. No. 10395. Joined Regular Army before 1914.

SMITH, ALEXANDER, 56 Milton Row. Private, 1st A. & S. Hrs. No. 9009. Joined August 1914.

SMITH, ALEXANDER, 57A Milton Row. Private, 13th Royal Scots. No. 16978. Joined January 1915.

SMITH, ALEXANDER P., 79A Milton Row. Private, Dorsetshire. No. 12766. Joined January 1916. *Killed.*

SMITH, DANIEL, 56 Milton Row. Private, 12th A. & S. Hrs. No. 6473. Joined November 1914. *Killed in action.*

SMITH, DAVID, 214 Stirling Street. Private, A. & S. Hrs. No. 26618. Joined June 1918.

SMITH, GEORGE, 56 Broad Street, Denny. Private, 4th Worcester Regiment. No. 53172. Joined September 1914.

SMITH, GEORGE, 80 Stirling Street. 2nd Lieutenant, K.O.S.B. Joined November 1914.

SMITH, HUGH, Stoneywood. Able Seaman, R.N.V. Reserve. No. C/Z5595. Joined June 1915.

SMITH, JAMES, 6 Rosebank, Dunipace. Private, A. & S. Hrs. No. 5849. Joined August 1914.

SMITH, JAMES, 85 Broad Street. Private, A. & S. Hrs. No. 5854. Joined October 1914.

SMITH, JOHN, 56 Milton Row, Dunipace. Private, 8th Royal Scots Fusiliers. No. 14563. Joined August 1914.

SMITH, JOSEPH, 56 Milton Row, Dunipace. Gunner, R.G.A. No. 196449. Joined November 1914.

Tears may be ours, but proud, for those who win
Death's royal purple in the foeman's lines.

LOWELL.

SMITH, PATRICK, 70A Broad Street. Private, Royal Dublin Fusiliers. No. 18111. Joined January 1915.

SMITH, ROBERT, 56 Milton Row. Private, 1st Royal Scots. No. 10182. Joined December 1907. Regular.

*SMITH, THOMAS, 67 Stirling Street. Private, 2nd Batt. Seaforths. No. 8784. Reservist. *Killed in action.*

SMITH, THOMAS B., Viewfield. Private, 2nd R.S.D., R.A.S.C. No. 295077.

SMITH, WILLIAM, 149 East Borland. Private, 13th Royal Scots. No. 34010. Joined February 1916.

SNEDDON, ALEXANDER, 15 West Borland Road. Private, A. & S. Hrs. No. 6842. Joined November 1914.

SNEDDON, DAVID, 127 Stirling Street. Private, A. & S. Hrs. No. 275972. Joined 1914.

SPACKMAN, ALEXANDER, 22 Glasgow Road. Private, R.A.F. No. 326803. Joined January 1919.

SPACKMAN, JAMES, 22 Glasgow Road. Private, Black Watch. No. 5940. Joined September 1914.

STANNERS, A. U., 34A Stirling Street. T.M.B., L.D. Artillery. No. 221487. Joined February 1917.

STANNERS, ADAM, 99 Stirling Street. Gunner, R.F.A. No. 218117. Joined December 1915.

STANNERS, GEORGE C., 99 Stirling Street. Private, Seaforth Hrs. No. S/28153. Joined June 1918.

STANNERS, WILLIAM D. C., 99 Stirling Street. Stoker, R.N. No. K/33168. Joined May 1916.

STARK, JAMES G., 10 Broad Street. Sergt., R.A.F. No. 22397. Joined February 1916.

STEWART, ALEXANDER, Lynemore, Denny. Private, 1st Batt. Cameron Hrs. No. 6101. Joined Sept. 1914. *Killed in action.*

*STEWART, ALEXANDER, 30 Broad Street. Private, A. & S. Hrs. No. 276322. Joined May 1915. *Killed in action.*

*STEWART, GEORGE, 42 Springfield Road. Sapper, R.E. No. 296205. Joined 1915. *Killed in action.*

STEWART, JOHN D., 122 Stirling Street. Co. Sergt.-Major, 17th Corp, C. Batt. No. 14045. Joined November 1914.

STEWART, JOHN R., 61 Stirling Street. Private, Cameron Hrs. No. 17160. Joined 1916. *Killed in action.*

We must be free or die, who speak the tongue
That Shakespeare spake—the faith and morals hold
Which Milton held.

WORDSWORTH.

STEWART, RICHARD HOPE, 21 Duke Street. L/Sergeant, 1st Northumberland Fusiliers. No. 46808. Joined November 1915.

STIRLING, CHARLES, 123 Stirling Street. Private, R.G.A. No. 129234. Joined 1916.

†STOCKS, ANDREW, 131 Stirling Street. Private, 2nd K.O.S.B. No. 16889. Joined November 1914. *Military Medal.*

STOCKS, LAURENCE, 92 Stirling Street. Private, 7th A. & S. Hrs. No. 1864. Joined August 1914.

STOCKS, WILLIAM T., 201 Stirling Street. C.Q.-M. Sergt., H.L.I. No. 9429. Joined September 1914. *D.C.M.*

STRACHAN, HENRY, 72 Duke Street. Gunner, R.G.A. No. 145003. Joined March 1917.

†STRACHAN, JAMES, 34 Fankerton. Sergt., Gordon Hrs. No. 6798. Joined November 1914. *Distinguished Conduct Medal, Military Medal, Meritorious Service Medal.*

STRACHAN, LEWIS, 78 Duke Street. Sergt., A. & S. Hrs. No. 2511. Joined August 1914.

STRACHAN, WILLIAM, 153 Stirling Street. Private, Cameron Hrs. No. 24029. Joined 1916.

SWEENEY, ANTHONY, 20 Broad Street. Private, Labour Corps. No. 644293. Joined August 1916.

SWEENEY, PATRICK, 46 Herbertshire Street. Private, R.D. Fusiliers. No. 18110. Joined 1915. *Killed in action.*

†TAYLOR, ALEXANDER L., 16 Herbertshire Street. Sergt., Scots Guards. No. 7265. Reservist 1914. *Military Medal.*

TAYLOR, DAVID, Backdales. Rifleman, Scottish Rifles. No. 41699.

*TENNANT, DANIEL, 21 Milton Row, Dunipace. Private, 6th Dorsets. No. 12768. Joined January 1915. *Killed.*

THOMSON, HUGH R., Carronbank, Denny. Corporal, 2nd Batt. Scots Guards. No. 9272. Joined 1914. *Prisoner of war in Germany.*

THOMSON, JAMES, 28 Milton Row, Dunipace. Private, 10th A. & S. Hrs. No. 1493. Joined August 1914.

*THOMSON, JAMES, 208 Stirling Street. Private, A. & S. Hrs. No. 6987. Joined November 1914. *Killed in action.*

Come to me in my dreams and then
By day I shall be well again!
For then the night will more than pay
The hopeless longing of the day.

MATTHEW ARNOLD.

THOMSON, JAMES, Heronfield, Denny. Sapper, R.E. No. 49986. Joined September 1914. *Killed in action.*

THOMSON, JAMES, 142 Stirling Street. Private, 3rd Batt. Royal Scots Fusiliers. No. 53275. Joined June 1918.

THOMSON, JOHN, Stirling Street, Denny. Corporal, 1/7th A. & S. Hrs. No. 40472. *Missing.*

THOMSON, JOHN, 6 Dryburgh Terrace. Corporal, R.A.F. No. 19806. Joined May 1915.

THOMSON, WILLIAM D., Milton Row, Dunipace. Private, A. & S. Hrs. No. 6467. Joined November 1914.

THURSBY, ROBERT, 10 Stirling Street. Private, Cameron Hrs. No. 25925. Joined 1916. *Killed in action.*

TODD, JOHN, 111A Stirling Street. Able Seaman, "Auson" Batt., R.N.D. No. Z/5135. Joined May 1915.

†*TUNSTALL, JOHN, Quarter House. Sergt., 1/7th A. & S. Hrs. No. 277353. Joined June 1916. *Killed in action. Military Medal.*

TURNBULL, DAVID, 3 Kilbirnie Close. Private, 12th A. & S. Hrs. No. 4582. Joined September 1914.

TURNBULL, HENRY, 3 Rosebank Court. Private, 2nd A. & S. Hrs. No. 9376. Joined February 1904. *Prisoner of war in Germany.*

TURNBULL, HENRY, 18 East Borland, Denny. Private, 7th A. & S. Hrs. No. 1569. Joined March 1912. *Killed in action.*

TURNBULL, HENRY, 79A Union Terrace. Private, 7th Royal Warwickshire. No. 5716. Joined April 1915. *Killed in action.*

TURNBULL, NEIL, 45 Broad Street. Private, A. & S. Hrs. No. 3558. Joined December 1914.

TURNBULL, WILLIAM, 45 Broad Street. Private, R.W.K. No. 1187. Joined September 1914.

TURNBULL, WILLIAM, 15 East Borland. L/Corporal, R.E. No. 198089. Joined April 1915.

TYSON, HINDLE, 45 Glasgow Road. Private, Worcestershire Regt. No. 45837. Joined January 1915.

VIRTUE, WILLIAM J., West Borland, Denny. Private, 1st A. & S. Hrs. No. 979. Joined 1910.

We'll hear nae mair lilting at the ewe milking;
Women and bairns are heartless and wae,
Sighing and moaning on ilka green loaning,
The Flowers of the Forest are a' wede away.

J. ELLIOTT.

WALKER, ARCHIBALD F., 1 Park Place. Private, 7th A. & S. Hrs. No. 1166. Joined January 1909.

WALKER, COMYN, 62 Boghead Place. Private, 7th Seaforth Hrs. No. 28122. Joined June 1918.

*WALKER, HENRY, Stripeside, Denny. Private, 5th Cameron Hrs. No. 22467. Joined April 1916. *Killed in action.*

WALKER, JAMES, Springfield Road, Denny. Private, A. & S. Hrs. No. 275330. Joined February 1914.

WALKER, JOHN, Springfield Road, Denny. Private, A. & S. Hrs. No. 276217. Joined August 1914.

WALKER, ROBERT, 61 Stirling Street. L/Corporal, H.L.I. No. 18801. Joined September 1914.

WALKER, THOMAS, 10 Bridgend Place. Private, Scottish Rifles. No. 15473. Joined 1917.

WALKER, WILLIAM, Springfield Road. Seaforth Hrs. No. 40634. Joined March 1915.

WALLACE, WILLIAM, Townfoot, Denny. Gunner, R.F.A. No. 192791. Joined January 1917.

WALLER, THOMAS, 8 West Borland Road. Private, 3rd Scottish Rifles. No. 32878. Joined April 1917.

*WATERS, ALEXANDER, 1 Kilbirnie Close. Corporal, Royal Scots. No. 15307. Joined September 1914. *Killed in action.*

WATTERS, GAVIN, Chasefield, Denny. Private, A. & S. Hrs. No. 15976.

WEAVER, JOHN, 2a Carron Terrace. Private, London Fusiliers. No. 17819. Joined March 1915.

†WEIR, GEORGE, 11 Davies Row. Private, 7th A. & S. Hrs. No. 275329. Joined February 1914. *Military Medal and Bar.*

WEIR, PETER D., 32 Broad Street. Private, A. & S. Hrs. No. 5750. Joined October 1914.

WEIR, THOMAS, 11 Davies Row. Private, 6th Cameron Hrs. No. 41257. Joined June 1916.

WEIR, WALTER, 7 East Borland Square. Private, 3/7 A. & S. Hrs. No. 4681. Joined December 1915.

WEIR, WILLIAM, 16 East Borland Place. Private, 10/11th H.L.I. No. 18286. Joined January 1915. *Killed in action.*

WEIR, WILLIAM, 1 Rosebank Court, Dunipace. Corporal, 1st A. & S. Hrs. No. 5210. Joined April 1915.

In the rent hearts of the people you will find treasures, golden treasures, of courage, steadfastness, devotion, and of faith that endureth for ever.

D. Lloyd George.

WESTWATER, JOHN, 61 Stirling Street. Driver, 416th Batt. R.F.A. No. 250757. Joined June 1918.

WESTWATER, PETER, 75A Union Terrace, Denny. Private, 6th Royal Munster Fusiliers. No. 1233. Joined September 1914.

WESTWATER, ROBERT, 75A Union Terrace, Denny. Private, 52nd Gordon Hrs. No. 30757. Joined July 1918.

WESTWATER, WILLIAM, Junr., 75A Union Terrace. L/Corporal, 14th H.L.I. No. 20953. Joined January 1915.

WHELTON, JOHN, 20 Broad Street. Private, A. & S. Hrs. No. 1495. Joined August 1914.

WHITE, ANDREW H., Stoneywood House. Driver, R.F.A. No. 218118. Joined December 1915.

WHITE, HENRY G., Stoneywood, Denny. Private, 17th Royal Scots. No. 38241. Joined November 1916.

WHITEHEAD, GEORGE, 104 Broad Street. Private, A. & S. Hrs. No. 26409. Joined June 1918.

WHITEHEAD, THOMAS, East Borland Square. Private, Labour Corps. No. 5258. Joined August 1915.

WHYTE, ALEXANDER T., Herbertshire Lodge. Private, Royal Scots Greys. No. 6288. Joined March 1906. Reservist.

WHYTE, ERNEST, Meadowbank, Holehouse. Lieutenant, R.F.C. *Killed in action.*

WHYTE, FRANK, 24 Glasgow Road. L/Corporal, Machine Gun Corps. No. 11864. Joined November 1915.

WHYTE, ROBERT, 24 Glasgow Road. L/Corporal, Gordon Hrs. No. 8526. Joined January 1915. *Killed in action.*

WILLIAMSON, ALEXANDER, 111 Stirling Street. Private, Cameron Hrs. No. 33245. Joined June 1918.

*WILLIAMSON, JOHN C., 13 Fankerton, Denny. L/Corporal, R.S.F. No. 22450. Joined December 1915. *Died in hospital (Scotland) after discharge.*

WILSON, ALEXANDER, Herbertshire Street. Private, 12th H.L.I. No. 18787. Joined August 1915. *Killed in action.*

WILSON, ANDREW, 54 Broad Street. Private, 4th Seaforth Hrs. No. 28372. Joined June 1918.

WILSON, DAVID, 149 East Borland Square. Private, A. & S. Hrs. No. 9248. Joined July 1903.

The whole wide ether is the eagle's way. The whole earth is a brave man's fatherland.

EURIPIDES.

WILSON, JOHN, 27 Fankerton, Denny. Able Seaman, "Drake" Batt. R.N.D. No. R/2145. Joined October 1914.

WILSON, JOHN, 28 Milton Row. Private, R.E. No. 157782.

WOOD, WILLIAM, 11 Lairox Terrace. Gunner, R.F.A. No. 167270. Joined December 1915.

WRIGHT, JAMES, 160 Wellstrand, Denny. L/Corporal, 10th A. & S. Hrs. No. 10724. Joined February 1908. *Killed in action.*

WRIGHT, JAMES, Gogarfield. Corporal, R.A.F. No. 28974. Joined November 1915.

WRIGHT, JOHN, 9 Hamilton Place. Private, 12th A. & S. Hrs. No. 5997. Joined October 1914. *Died of wounds.*

WRIGHT, WILLIAM, Helenbank, Denny. Private, H.L.I. No. 43299. Joined November 1914. *Died in Germany, prisoner of war.*

WYNESS, JOHN, 53A Milton Row, Dunipace. Private, R.E. No. 343430. Joined March 1918.

WYNESS, LESLIE, 53A Milton Row, Dunipace. Private, Royal Scots Fusiliers. No. 48539. Joined November 1914.

WYNESS, PETER, 234 Stirling Street. Private, A. & S. Hrs. No. 27766. Joined April 1916.

YOUNG, WILLIAM, Anchor View. Private, A. & S. Hrs. No. 6481. Joined 1914.

The Monument, a sketch of which appears as the frontispiece of the Roll of Honour, is the work of G. H. Paulin, A.R.S.A., Glasgow. The pedestal is of grey granite, and the bronze figure of Victory or Peace has been adopted from the Burgh Seal. The site of the Monument, a knoll to the east of Denny Cemetery, is the gift of Charles William Forbes, Esq., of Callendar.

The illustration of the Monument is reproduced from a sketch by the sculptor. Herbertshire Castle has been photographed from a drawing by Miss Sherriff, Carronvale, in "Lands and Lairds of Larbert and Dunipace Parishes." The photograph of the moulding shop at Denny Iron Works was taken by Bailie James K. Shanks, Managing Director. The photograph of the machine in Carrongrove Paper Mill is by George A. Skinner, Fankerton. All the other photographs are by David Ritchie, newsagent, Denny. The paper on which the Roll is printed is the gift of the Carrongrove Paper Company, Limited.

BANKS & CO. LTD., EDINBURGH.